I0817568

THE POCKET BOOK OF
PLATO

THE POCKET BOOK OF PLATO

MICHAEL MOORE

Picture credits
Shutterstock: 9, 13, 20, 25, 31, 41, 46, 48, 50 (x2), 53, 58, 65, 68 (x2), 75, 83, 86, 94, 104, 108, 118, 120, 140, 146, 148, 150, 152 (x2), 157, 166, 175, 181, 186, 189, 190, 195

Wikimedia Commons: 44 (x2)

This edition published in 2025 by Sirius Publishing, a division of Arcturus Publishing Limited,
26/27 Bickels Yard, 151–153 Bermondsey Street,
London SE1 3HA

ISBN: 978-1-3988-5127-6
AD011627US

Printed in China

Contents

Chapter 1

INTRODUCTION

Plato was the top dog leading all of them, a sweet-speaking preacher, as musical as the cicadas, sitting on a tree in the Academy and sending forth a voice as beautiful as a lily.

Timon, 4th–3rd century BC poet

Plato, disciple of Socrates, teacher of Aristotle, through an ancestry including Solon the great lawgiver of Athens, was born in that ancient city in 427 BC. Of his early life there is little known, and an equal amount worth mentioning. He was educated by a certain Dionysius while also learning the customary Athenian care of the body at the gymnasium. Apparently he excelled at the physical, as his name, "Platon," (anglicized to "Plato,") means "broad" and its most credible explanation comes as praise for his stout body. Other possibilities put forth for the origin of his "broad" name include a wide forehead and a magnanimous breadth of style in his writing.

When he was 20 he came to study with Socrates until that philosopher's impactful death when Plato was around 28. He studied widely with different philosophers after Socrates' death, and he traveled extensively, including time in Egypt. At some point returning to Athens he set up shop in an old gymnasium named after the hero Academus. We now know this spot as the Academy, and it is this location which would serve as a school and headquarters for the vast array of Plato's intellectual activities.

Plato.

Even in his own time Plato must have been an intellectual of repute, as we not only have reports of high initial attendance at his public lecture, *On the Good*, but also he is the only author from antiquity whose work we possess entire. Of his works, there are a series of 13 letters purported to be by Plato, written to various political leaders, most importantly Syracusan tyrants, but which have long been suspected to have been written by others, except for the seventh. The seventh is full of biographical information including Plato's motivations for not pursuing a political career and his coyness about his sharing the full teaching of his philosophy.

The real legacy of Plato resides in his dialogues, where Socrates often takes center stage as the main character. The dialogues of Plato are usually thought to begin with the *Apology*. This work is not technically a dialogue since it is a report of Socrates' defense at his trial for corruption. But it is here that one can appreciate the love Plato felt for his master. Because of the size of Plato's literary output there is a long tradition of differing ways to organize the dialogues. One of the more popular methods in antiquity was to sort the dialogues by type, for example, concerning the ethical or tentative or inconclusive. Frequently modern interpreters have chosen to arrange the dialogues by chronology, deciding on the order by internal clues and certain assumptions about Plato's development as a thinker.

The Life of Plato

431 BC – Peloponnesian War begins

428/427 BC – Plato Born

406/405 BC – Plato enrolled as Athenian Citizen

404 BC – Peloponnesian War ends

399 BC – Socrate's Trial and Death

390s BC – Plato begins philosophical writing
~399–387 BC – Travels abroad— Southern Italy, Egypt, Phoenicia
387 BC – Founds Academy
384 BC – Meets Dion and Dionysius I in Syracuse, Sicily
367 BC – Meets Aristotle
366–365 BC – Second trip to Syracuse
361–360 BC – Third trip to Syracuse
347 BC – Death of Plato

Major Works

There are a few dozen works which most scholars accept as authentic, while other texts, such as most of his attributed epistles, are considered spurious. The *Republic* would have to stand at the head of the list of his most famous works, for in this mammoth dialogue Plato engages with ethics, politics, metaphysics, knowledge, and more. Next in order of prominence is the *Phaedo*, which is dramatically set when Socrates is awaiting his execution, another rich dialogue concerning immortality and the fear of death. The *Meno* is a captivating dialogue about

Plato's Key Ideas

Discussed in	Topic	Major Theme	Dialogues
Chapter 2	Love	A desire to possess the good forever	*Symposium*
Chapter 3	Poetry	Poetry as a persuasive, influential force	*Ion*, *Republic*
Chapter 4	Socratic Elenchus	Testing truth	Early Dialogues, *Gorgias*, *Protagoras*
Chapter 5	Immortal Soul	Immortality and the three parts of the soul	*Phaedo*
Chapter 6	Virtue is Knowledge	Correct knowledge is correct action	*Meno*, *Protagoras*
Chapter 7	Theory of Forms	Forms account for knowledge and existence	*Parmenides*, *Phaedo*, *Phaedrus*
Chapter 8	Two Worlds	Reconciliation of change and stability	*Republic*
Chapter 9	Gods	Piety is the correct understanding of the gods	*Laws*, *Theaetetus*, *Timaeus*, *Phaedo*

Chapter 10	The Good	The good is that at which everything aims	*Philebus*
Chapter 11	Politics	The structure of the city mirrors the soul	*Republic*

the theory of knowledge and reincarnation. Several dialogues engage the various issues having to do with rhetoric and speech; some engaging sophistry, such as *Protagoras* and *Gorgias*, one on rhetoric, *Phaedrus*, and a speculative work on the origin and function of language, *Cratylus*. *Timaeus*, a creative work of speculation, which centers on the creation and makeup of the universe, was highly influential in the Middle Ages. The *Symposium* on love, the *Apology*, a record of Socrates' court trial, and the *Euthyphro*, concerning piety and justice, round out the most lasting of his works in the popular imagination. However, Plato's most rigorously philosophical influence, his distinct contributions to scholarly work, loom just as large, with *Parmenides* a master class in abstract logic,

Theatetus a discussion of the nature of knowledge, and *Sophist* concerning the nature of being.

The scope of Plato's work is staggeringly wide (remember this is one of the explanations for his name, "Broad") and this has contributed to much speculation about Plato's own convictions. The dialogue form—and Plato himself never appears as a character—generally prevents us from determining what Plato himself thought about the subjects under discussion. Some have attempted to get around this problem by attributing Plato's views to Socrates, but this invites added difficulties to whatever solutions it provides.

Influences on Plato

Interest in Plato's own views has also naturally found another source which is at least as promising as attempting to extract them from the dialogues. This is to look to Plato's own influences outside of Socrates. There is substantial evidence within the dialogues that Plato has borrowed from Pythagoras, a mystic philosopher, and shown admiration for the philosophical and religious sect he founded. The most immediately noticeable of these Pythagorean influences is the doctrine of the transmigration of the soul, more commonly known as reincarnation. Of no less importance was Pythagoras' emphasis that numbers were the ultimate reality behind everything, an idea which Plato not only adapted in his unique way, but more generally pushed him to look to causes and explanations which were non-physical, just as numbers themselves.

The rich complexity of Plato's philosophy owes to him engaging with the tensions in his predecessors' thoughts. So for example, in Parmenides he recognized a thinker who claimed that everything was one, while in Heraclitus everything was always changing. It was Plato's introduction of Forms which was an attempt to unite these disparate ideas.

Plato's Rivals

One would be mistaken, however, to think that Plato was merely engaged in borrowing and reconciling the philosophical ideas swirling about in his own time. There were entire groups of people with whom Plato was engaged in ideological battle, whose influence he was attempting to check and ideas he adamantly argued against. These were the poets whose works help, he thought, to corrupt the youth, and the sophists, itinerant "wise men," who would teach anyone to speak on any topic (and win any argument), for the right fee. Plato went to great lengths to correct and rebut the ideas he found promoted by these thinkers, penning entire dialogues on these subjects. Some of the more important ideas were the theme of imitation, the existence of truth, the nature of virtue, and the features of knowledge.

Additionally, Plato was fighting against the influence of the sophists. These capable "wise men" were something like legal mercenaries whose skills Plato, at least judged through Socrates in the dialogues, was no fan of. There are a handful of Platonic dialogues named after actual sophists, *Protagoras* and *Gorgias*, and the sophists are engaged in many dialogues, directly or indirectly. One of the main claims these itinerant teachers made is that they possessed knowledge of everything and furthermore, that this knowledge could be communicated and taught to anyone, for a price.

A last group of antagonists are the rhetoricians and speech writers. In that classical age, an Athenian who was taken into court could have his speech written on his behalf. One of the more famous of these speechwriters, Lysias, is prominent in the dialogue *Phaedrus*, as the beginning of the dialogue is an exercise in picking apart one of his compositions. Isocrates, in Plato's own time, was an explicit rival. He attempted to showcase his own model of education, centered on the study of humane rhetoric, at the expense of Plato's own focus on philosophy. Isocrates even used the term "philosophy" to describe what he was doing—an association of "love of wisdom" quite different than what we think of as Plato's activities.

Politics and Sicily

A crucial piece of Plato's biographical background concerns his visits to Sicily. These are noteworthy because they indicate Plato's interest in actually effecting a practical political scheme, and because we have inherited certain letters which are purported to have been written by the philosopher himself as a record of his affairs there. The outline of the most relevant details is that Dionysius was a tyrant of Syracuse, though it was with his brother, Dion, that Plato truly hit it off. After Dionysius the younger took over after his father's death some decades later, Plato was once again invited to institute political reform, largely under the influence of Dion. He was hindered in this opportunity, as Dion was soon exiled by the young Dionysius and Plato's association with Dion only strengthened Dionysius' resistance to Plato. After unsuccessfully attempting to have Dion recalled, Plato left Sicily once again.

Socrates and Plato

Any book on Plato must address the central interpretive question about Plato's own views and those of Socrates. Apart from Xenophon's account of the life and philosophy of Socrates, we do not really have a robust record of Socrates as a philosopher. Add to this the fact that Xenophon's contributions have been totally eclipsed by Plato's influence, and we are left with the difficult question of where Socrates ends and Plato begins. As interesting as the

Socrates, Plato's teacher and friend.

answers to that question can be, it is not the purpose of this book. This book looks to what Plato said in his existing writings, and whether he places words in the mouth of Socrates which are not his own, but undoubtedly the words of Plato. He has written words and we, his audience, read them. This is no different, in principle, from discussing Shakespeare without regard to the difficulties in separating his own convictions from those of his characters and without making a decision on the historical identity of the author. At any rate, we will be sticking to the text, identifying important and repeated themes in the entirety of Plato's extant writing.

The Manuscript History of Plato

Plato's corpus, is something of a miracle. As mentioned at the beginning of this introduction, he is the only author whose work exists entire. We know this from lists compiled in antiquity, telling us that we are missing large parts, or sometimes the entire output, of extremely important ancient authors.

What is really illuminating is that the fascination with Plato's philosophy, his creativity, wit, persuasion, characters, questions, answers, insights, discussions, and arguments has gripped on our collective imagination for over two millennia. This is the real reason why scribes have been copying him for so long.

Besides the preservation of his texts, the next most important features of the texts themselves are their division into tetralogies. This was done by a philosopher named Thrasyllus in the 1st century AD. By arranging the works of Plato into nine groups of four, or tetralogies, "Thrasyllus' canon" influenced the way that Plato's work has been read for centuries. His arrangement included placing the *Euthyphro* and *Apology* first and the *Letters* last.

Interpreting Plato

Through the centuries there have been many different interpretive schools of Plato. Even within Plato's own Academy, the successors to his philosophy disagreed with what the old master said. Some read the dialogues with a skeptical bent, thinking that Plato was urging us toward this approach with Socratic questioning. Others still find in them dogmatic pronouncements dear to Plato's heart. So-called Neo-Platonism elevated the spiritual elements found in Plato's work, and taking the notion of a supreme Unity and Goodness made it into something of a god. As for this book, we are taking a view that what is said in the dialogues and letters is fair game to speak on its own. That is, it is "Platonic" in the same sense that anything said in one of Shakespeare's plays is "Shakespearean." The texts have much to say, and in the following ten chapters we will explore some of the more dominant themes in Plato, from love to politics, and everything in between.

Chapter 2

LOVE

"My main point is that every desire for good things, and for happiness, is the 'greatest love, and a deceitful love, for everyone.' But all those people who are turned to love in all variety of ways either by yearning for money or exercise or wisdom are neither said to be 'loving' nor are they called 'lovers,' but only those who go after one particular kind of love with zeal possess the name of the whole of love, as 'love,' and 'loving' and 'lovers.'"

Diotima, *Symposium*, 205d1–6

In this passage from Plato's *Symposium*, Diotima, the mysterious priestess, relates an insight about the nature of love. Men have been called to a dinner party at the house of Agathon the poet, and take turns in praising Eros, the god of love. When it comes to Socrates' turn, he relates the insights that he gained from the direct tutelage of Diotima. On her telling, romantic or erotic love, as we may name it, is but one variety of the broader category of love. All loves are a kind of longing, a desire to possess something, whether it is already possessed or will be. This desire to possess always concerns good things not bad things. The nature of love is turned toward the good. What is characteristic of romantic love in particular is that it is the most powerful manifestation of this general phenomenon we call "love."

Love is something we all experience, yet apart from the experience of the powerful pull itself, few can explain what it is. But whatever this ever-present force in human life is, we aspire to its euphoric clutch and praise it when we find it.

In the *Symposium* dialogue what is revealed to us is that love necessarily involves several important elements, some of which like desire and beauty are obvious, while with others like immortality and the good it is more difficult at first to see their direct connection to love.

In this chapter we will discover that love is a desire for good things, and that these "good things," a term which captures a great variety of objects, are something we both seek after and wish to possess forever. Love, due to the nature of its objects, draws in goodness, beauty, and immortality in the scope of its desire. The move toward immortality might be the most surprising of all these associations, for the reason that for Plato it is impossible for there to be love without the pull to immortality.

An Ancient Greek symposium scene from c.480 BC.

Love and the Good

"Diotima asked, 'And what will there be for the man who has good things?'
'I am able to answer this more easily,' I said, '—he will be happy.'
Diotima replied, 'Yes, for the happy are happy *because of the possession of their good things* and it is no longer necessary to ask why a man wishing to be happy wishes to be happy.'"

Diotima and Socrates, *Symposium* 204e3–205a3

This quotation highlights the significance of the idea of the *good*. It is a common occurrence in Plato that the good is desirous, whether something is actually good, or its goodness is apparent, and mistakenly thought to be good. This makes sense of the idea that we humans pursue immortality through reproduction, because we think immortality is good. The good is in one sense whatever it is we desire, for whenever we are desiring something, from the Platonic point of view, we think we are pursuing something good. No one pursues what is bad, at least knowingly, according to this line of thinking.

The distinction between the actually good and the merely good gives rise to another concept, which will be explored more fully in chapter 10: *the Good*. Put briefly, Plato describes an ultimate Good that is beyond anything and everything. It explains all, and in a sense everything is striving toward this singular Good, even though in most circumstances people are led along by a particular, singular good. Many people do no not give a lot of thought to the life-long culmination of what we can call a happy life, but instead focus on what will make them happy in the moment. Yet this pursuit of the immediate presumably informs their pursuit of the long term, and likewise, our pursuit of the immediate good leads to the pursuit of the ultimately good.

Plato says that there is a direct relationship between our desire for the good and immortality. When we acquire something good, we want to hold on to it for as long as we can. We want to continue having that good thing forever, and that will require immortality.

There are two aspects to understand: first, we want our beloved object never to depart from us as long as we live. Second, we want this object of love to exist along with us for an everlasting period of time. These two features of immortality attract us as we experience the desire called love. The first is immortality taken on its own, a prized good to be sought out because it is something divine, properly possessed by the gods. The second aspect of immortality is that anything else we deem a good, we want to possess eternally. We both want to live forever, for our own sake, after the model of the gods, and we want to possess goods, and with this goodness in our possession we wish to enjoy them forever.

"And it is necessary that when the good is desired there is also desire for immortality, when there is a love for the good *for oneself*."

Symposium, 207a1–2

TWO ELEMENTS OF IMMORTALITY

TRUE IMMORTALITY	
↗	↖
Desire for the preservation of the self	Desire for the self's good

Immortality, importantly, is not naked; it is sought out so that it can be enjoyed with other goods. We pursue it not merely for itself, but insofar as it is connected to what is good. We do not want to be eternally wicked or live a life of immortality surrounded by what is bad. Following the gods means not only being immortal but being good.

In the case of animals such as humans are, we must constantly replenish what we participate in. Diotima gives as an example: the case of knowledge. We must apply ourselves to reacquiring knowledge since we are forgetful creatures. When it comes to immortality, we must occasionally refresh our share in it, and this means that we must reproduce.

Diotima broadens this concept to drive home the point that the mortal is always changing and the immortal is always the same. This suggests that what is always changing seeks to attain the state of always being the same. The mortal seeks the immortal, the human seeks the divine, what changes seeks what does not. This again goes back to the idea that we want to possess what is good forever. Yet, we humans are in a precarious spot if we are limited to pursuing the immortal only through the process of reproduction. We are stuck with attempting to become immortal through reproducing more of our kind, but this activity never achieves personal immortality. It is as if we are doomed to an activity which never satisfies but always draws us in desire.

One important difference that Diotima acknowledges is the notion that mortal things are always changing, while the realm of the divine or unseen is not. This is no mere difference, as the fact that the divine realm does not change is manifestly superior to our earthly realm which does. Humans seek the immortal not only because to do so is to enter into a state where we can always possess what we have, but also because the divine realm of unchangingness is superior to the flux of our world.

Love and Beauty

Beauty serves in some ways as the ultimate aim of our love, since the good is that which is more beautiful than anything else. "The beautiful is good and the good is beautiful" is in fact a fundamental principle of Plato. Diotima tells us that people seek to "give birth in beauty." The phrase is ambiguous, but whatever else it involves, it requires that beauty is the focus of our desire, not ugliness. Perhaps unsurprisingly beauty is characterized as in "harmony" with the divine. The nature of the beautiful, in harmony with the divine, is what draws animals and humans alike to reproduce, since they come nearer the immortality that the divine possesses. One point that comes across in the use of this language is we are not talking about literal distance and space in approaching the gods. Perhaps we could say that we come closer to the gods in our nature, or that we approach in degree what we could never completely achieve. But beauty by itself is not quite what human beings are after, Diotima tells us. The beauty, remember, must be secured, just like any other good, forever.

The true beauty we are after is not the mere physical beauty we experience in the here and now. The beauty here is just a token of the true beauty which is beyond our physical senses. This should not be entirely surprising. During this entire exposition Diotima has been spiritualizing what is, on first appearances, a very physical and biological act. Love is ultimately not pursued for the satisfaction of our biological needs, but this desire of our bodily need points us toward something much greater.

Love and Immortality

The immortality that Socrates and Diotima discuss in the dialogue is quite literally the lack of death. On this understanding one simply wishes to live without life ever coming to an end. As Plato depicts it, mortals contrast strongly in this way with the immortal gods, since humans are thrust into a situation where they first come into being, birth. So humans are mortal creatures who possess a desire to become like the gods in this way. But the ultimate fulfillment of this desire is not available to human creatures. The human desire is stoked by the example of the immortality of the gods, but since only the gods are immortal by nature, humans have to make do with daisy chaining themselves, in a manner of speaking, into immortality. Humans attain this daisy chain by a process of reproduction. Each new human in turn gets to live their portion of mortality, and in turn can repeat this process to grant a new generation life once again, and the process continues on forever.

In one sense whether humans can actually achieve immortality is a question that one can put aside. Certainly, from Diotima's perspective, there is such a thing as immortality. But from another point of view the truth of immortality is less important than the insight that Plato gives us into human psychology. This insight amounts to the fact that humans do indeed seem to desire the furtherance of the species to which they belong. It is through modern technological interventions that we have come to dissociate sex from procreation, but such an innovation was not available to Plato or his audience.

This desire to continue living on, in the limited manner available to humans, through reproduction, is the explanation of love. This is what love, Eros, looks like, in broad strokes.

The Ladder of Love

After stressing the importance of our human striving to attain the divine and immortal, Diotima has in store another argument if what has been said so far has been unpersuasive. There must be something beyond the merely physical involved in biological reproduction. The reason is that despite the great importance we take in reproduction, or continuing our existence through having children, we do not behave as though this is the only way to achieve immortality. Sometimes we seek fame and glory, even when we ourselves and our children die in the process. These kinds of people are attracted to immortality outside of the typical physical avenue.

TYPES OF IMMORTALITY

Type	Possessed by	Achieved by
Unconditional	Gods	(Always possessed)
Conditional	Humans Animals Plants	Biological Reproduction Fame

This opens up the multiple ways that immortality is available to us, but there is a surprising wrinkle which Diotima adds. This is the famous Ladder of Love in the *Symposium*. This combines all the ideas we have seen so far in our discussion of love: immortality, desire, beauty, procreation, divinity.

If we were to sum up the Ladder of Love we would say a human, by moving from smaller to

larger portions of beauty, progresses in love until finally finding the ultimate Beauty, the beauty of beauties and the culmination of what all other beautiful things seek. Diotima reveals that there is a progression from the lesser to the greater, and from the more bodily to the less, and from the more concrete to the less. One must begin with the body of a single beautiful thing, loving this one particular person, then moving on to the bodies of two beautiful people. As she elaborates this ascent, the next progression is to all beautiful bodies, then

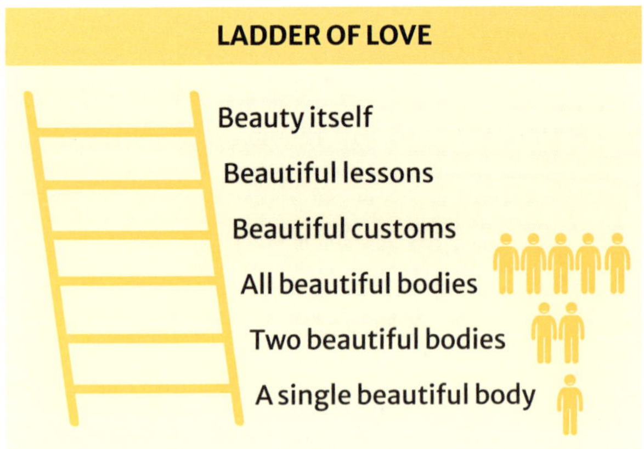

to beautiful customs, then to beautiful lessons. At the apex of this ladder is Beauty itself.

When the initiate has arrived at this vision of Beauty itself he comes to appreciate how real beauty never passes away and is always the same. Unlike our earthly experience with beauty, Beauty itself always looks the same no matter what perspective we view it from or how much time passes. Such is the attainment of this sight that one need only achieve it once, and after that, living in the light of this revelation of true Beauty, he is able to "give birth to beauty," not in any common way, but leading to immortality. The vision of this otherworldly beauty can be experienced by the inner eye alone, and it is this beauty which can never perish that calls us to follow after it everlastingly.

Chapter 3

POETRY

“In this more than anything I think the god has shown us, in order to avoid doubt, that these poems are not human nor even from humans, but they are godlike and come from the gods, and poets are nothing other than interpreters of the gods, possessed by whomever each poet is possessed by.”

Socrates in *Ion* 534e1–4

The Battle Between Philosophy and Poetry

Many are familiar with the Socrates parodied by the poet Aristophanes in *The Clouds*. Socrates comes across as an aloof and eccentric character, scarcely capable of profound insights as opposed to trivial sophisms. In Plato, on the other hand, there are several discussions of poets and poetry, neither of which come off very well. Plato refers to "an ancient quarrel between poetry and philosophy" in the last book of the *Republic*. What Plato focuses on in that dialogue is the dispute as to whether poetry has a place in the just city. To determine this, the content of poetry must be evaluated for knowledge. In the quotation we started with, Socrates is talking to Ion, the poet rhapsode. The conclusion he makes there is a good starting point for this discussion, for it too raises doubts about whether the poet brings knowledge to what he writes.

Poetry is a persuasive force for Plato. It enchants and convinces, and characteristically it turns people toward what is untrue. Poetry is an imitation of the actual world, and for this it presents the danger of illusion—mistaking a picture of the world for the world itself. Yet for all this, Plato also portrays poetry as something divine, a creation that is not so much human as divine in origin. The depiction of poetry in Plato is a mixed bag, dangerous and divine in its very nature. The importance of poetry for Plato centers on the authority of poetry as a form of knowledge. Is poetry a form of knowledge? Do poets possess

Ancient Greek poetry, starting with Homer, was a beautiful and persuasive form of art.

knowledge of what they talk about? Is poetry a rival form of knowledge to philosophy?

Poetry in Ancient Athens

In the culture of classical Athens poetry was influential and inescapable. In particular the figure of Homer and his poetry held a position of great power. The people looked to Homer for wisdom and advice, quite parallel to the way that the Bible provided unquestioned guidance in previous ages. It is Homer above all who will come into the crosshairs of Plato's pen and Socrates' mouth.

From Plato's perspective there was a battle over who ought to hold influence over the people of the city. He sagaciously does not frame it as a battle between philosophers and poets, but between philosophy and poetry—for it is a difficult task to bill oneself as directly competing against the illustrious Homer.

Expertise and Poetry

In *Ion*, Socrates meets up with a rhapsode of the same name, a professional reciter of Homeric poetry. He is interested in what kind of knowledge Ion possesses from his memorization and recitation of Homer. In general terms Socrates says that Homer explains how men deal with each other and with gods, and even how the gods interact with each other. But Socrates observes, with Ion agreeing, that Ion himself can only speak about how Homer addresses a given topic. In other words he cannot speak on the subject himself, for example, of riding chariots, as this subject is brought up in other poets. This shows that Ion does not have any actual knowledge of the subject he is discussing. If he did have knowledge of the subject, Socrates points out, then he would be able to discuss the topic no matter where it was found or who brought it up

The parallel Socrates draws to convince Ion, adapted to modern examples, Is the case of an expert in painting. Would we consider someone knowledgeable in the arena of painting, if he could explain what was good and notable in Da Vinci's *Mona Lisa*, but not in Van Gogh's self-portrait? Socrates answers that of course we would not think so, and this is the same in poetry.

POETRY

Expertise covers a whole field.

A capable artist can explain the beauty and skill of both paintings.

This is the point at which Socrates turns to a rather fascinating and famous comparison. Remember, Socrates has argued that Ion does not possess real knowledge, but he still has to explain how it is that Ion pulls off his recitations of Homer. Since poets use words, those words must come from somewhere, but it is not the intellect, for that is the domain of knowledge. Instead Socrates proposes that these words come through divine inspiration. It is a madness that overcomes the poet, as he is literally inspired by the gods, taken over by a divine possession he has no control over.

Magnetic Poetry

Socrates compares the way poetry works to magnets. Just as magnets transfer their power to iron, making the metal magnetized, but not as powerful as the magnet itself, so the Muse is able to inspire the poet to compose great poetry. Listeners in turn become a part of this noble cascade, transfixed, and as Socrates seems to imply, stupefied, by the process. The poet and his audience are both caught up in something beyond themselves because it originates outside of themselves, and are unable to give any reasonable account of it.

Unlike the account in the *Republic* we are going to turn to, this is arguably a mixed bag of praise and blame. There is criticism of poetry in that some of its practitioners apparently do not have knowledge, and from a philosopher's point of view, this is not something to be celebrated. But what we can say is that poetry is something divine, and this suggests that far from being bad, it should be praised and taken in the highest regard.

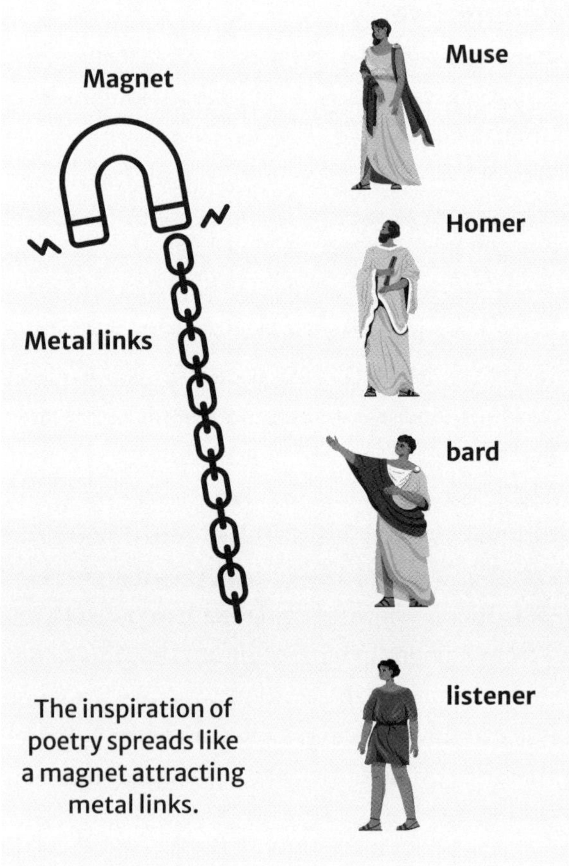
Magnet
Muse
Homer
Metal links
bard
listener
The inspiration of poetry spreads like a magnet attracting metal links.

The *Republic* and Poetry

In addition to *Ion* Plato also gives Socrates large sections of the *Republic* during which he critiques poetry from the perspective of creating a just city with just citizens. In book two Socrates raises the alarm on the disturbing depiction of the gods in the poetry. The worry here still begins with Homer, who portrays gods as engaging in very human-like behavior with, from Plato's perspective, appalling and repugnant results.

But Plato also brings up poetry for attack in two further books. In book three Socrates brings up the importance of moral formation in the lives of citizens. Poetry plays an outsized role in the development of habits and attitudes, especially among young people, and it was this concern that Plato had in mind in subjecting it to scrutiny. One interesting aspect of the theological meeting the practical is the poetical description of Hades. Within the *Republic* the traditional depiction of Hades is viewed as a bad thing, because it is a place of deprivation and despair. This means that soldiers will be cowardly in war to avoid death and this is a disastrous incentive for a

Hades.

political state needing to defend itself.

Socrates himself asks forgiveness from the poets for the censorship coming to all the poets.

"When it comes to these poems we will ask Homer and all the other poets not to become angry if we delete their verses, not because they are unpoetic or unpleasing to the masses, but inasmuch as they are more poetically crafted they should not be heard by children and men, who ought to be free rather than fearing the slavery of death."

Republic, 387b1–8

In book three the focus also turns to a distinction between two kinds of poetic method. One is narrative, the other is mimetic, where "mimetic" is just the

Greek word for imitation. Note that this is not the traditional division of poetry into lyric, epic, drama, and comedies and other subfields. Rather this is a distinction about the manner of presentation of poetry to the audience. From the *Republic*'s view of the matter, the content of a poetical work can be delivered in one of two ways, either with the poet making himself conspicuous or hiding himself.

Though this may seem inconsequential to us, the case that Socrates makes is that when a poet inserts himself straightforwardly into the poem itself as the relater of a story, he serves as a buffer between the fictional story and the audience. But if he fails to do this, the audience loses the necessary self-awareness and guardedness they need to avoid being deceived and drawn into bad behavior.

WHAT MAKES POETRY ACCEPTABLE

Type of Poetry	Acceptable	Why?
Narrative	Yes	Shows a distinction between narrator and characters
Mimetic	No	Blurs line between narrator and characters

We might draw a parallel here between our contemporary enjoyment of horror films and dramatic movies. Because there is no narrator of what is happening, we come to functionally put ourselves into the shoes of the characters we see. We are scared at what occurs in the movie, or moved to the point of despair at what we see unfolding before us. In

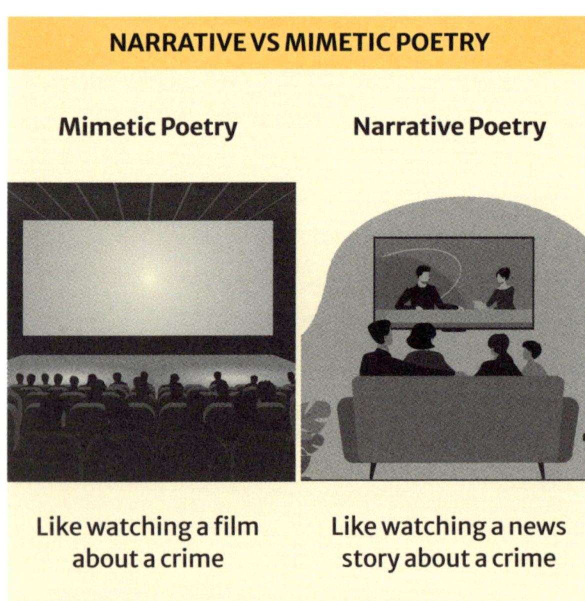

the process of experiencing and thinking through the different events being presented to us, we are influenced—for the worse—to imitate what we have seen. The habits of our minds in fiction become the habits of our actions in reality.

The last book of the *Republic* has the most weighty of the reasons to reject poetry. It is here that Plato broaches the subject of his infamous Forms (see Chapter 7). For temporary purposes we can say that a Form is a non-physical entity of some kind that is independent of the things we see in our world, but which gives the things in our world their very cause for existing. For instance, if there is such a thing as a cat, there is a Form of a Cat, and if there is such a thing as something good, there is a Form of Goodness.

Plato's most serious attack on poetry works from within this understanding of Forms. As Socrates explains, poetry is three places away from reality. In the example given in the *Republic*, the Form of a bed is the real bed, while the physical bed created by a carpenter is an imitation of that Form. In distant third is the bed that is depicted in painting or poetry, because at this point it is a copy of a copy.

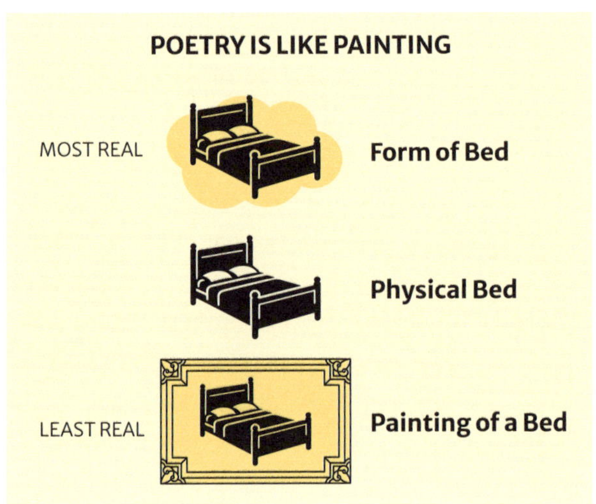

Poetry is the copy of human affairs which are themselves an imitation of the divine realm of the Forms. Poetry is a counterfeit, a derivative expression of what is perfect. Ultimately this will go some way to explain how poetry does not reflect adequately the nature of truth, simply owing to its origin as an imitation of an imitation. The farther away from the Form the farther away from what is good and true. Being separated from ultimate reality, in this way poetry is necessarily false.

As an example, consider a well-executed painting of a countryside. Even if the mountains, trees, and landscape are painted with the utmost skill, it will still be the case that the painting is a false image of the physical mountains and the real mountains that are beyond even this material manifestation. The painting, it needs to be pointed out, can never be a mountain. It has the appearance of being a mountain but only from the right perspective and distance, and

A landscape painting, no matter how accurate, is never an actual landscape.

it is never as convincing as the physical mountain, which is itself a copy.

Socrates also acknowledges that with the poet there is a great deal of danger in thinking he knows more than he does. In writing about everything, the poet gives the wrong impression to his listeners that he possesses a vast knowledge of things.

"It is necessary for a good poet, if he will compose a poem well concerning the topics he composes on, composes knowingly, or else he would not be able to compose at all."

Republic, 598e3–6

Poetry in Plato is actually afforded a great deal of respect. Poetry is acknowledged to have great cultural impact and Homer is treated as someone with authority. In fact, Plato sometimes quotes Homer when the poet says something that Plato or Socrates appears to be endorsing. In the final analysis, however, poetry is one of those competing intellectual fields, along with sophistry and rhetoric, to name two others, with which Plato was attempting to make some elbow room for the nascent field of philosophy.

Chapter 4

ELENCHUS

"And of what type of man am I? If I say anything false, I am of those who are pleased to be refuted, and in turn I am pleased to refute, if someone should speak anything false. Indeed I am not more unpleased to be refuted than to refute."

Socrates, *Gorgias*, 458a2–4

These are the words and self-description of Socrates and they have a way of striking the reader as quite odd, for they do not entirely align with our expectation of what a philosopher, or even Socrates, appears to do. The philosopher is highly disputatious and hankering for verbal confrontations so that he can win an argument. At least this is the stereotype, and some suspect Socrates plays dumb only in order to lull his sparring partners into a vulnerable position.

"Elenchus" is a word which denotes both "refuting" but also the less polemical "testing." It is an approach that we see Socrates employ in the early dialogues. The significance of elenchus cannot be overstated. The reason is that Socrates is in constant pursuit of knowledge through other people. He wants to see if other people know anything, and the only way to guarantee the

Gorgias, one of the foremost sophists of Ancient Athens, and the focus of a Platonic dialogue.

truth of what these people say is through a rigorous process of investigative conversation. Elenchus is a social engagement where the stakes are truth and knowledge. This exchange of ideas is fundamental to the nature of philosophy and its origin as a dialogue.

The Spirit of Philosophy

But this is not the way Socrates explains it nor how Plato portrays him. The spirit with which Socrates pursues philosophy is just as important as the conclusions he comes to. The Platonic depiction of the philosopher is one who is not interested in winning but in uncovering the truth. The dialogue from which the quotation on page 57 was taken, *Gorgias*, is a highly charged competitive atmosphere, with Socrates locking horns with Gorgias, the famous sophist. But Socrates is not interested in winning, at least from the standpoint of earning plaudits from bystanders or getting one over on Gorgias simply because he holds a view on the opposite side.

Socrates' interest lays in the truth and the investigative process by which the truth is uncovered. A philosophical dispute is often viewed as a tug of war between two irreconcilable views. But Plato's picture is that philosophy is necessarily a joint effort, where at least two parties are involved in the "hunt" for the truth. They both have something at stake, the resolution of their question, whatever it is.

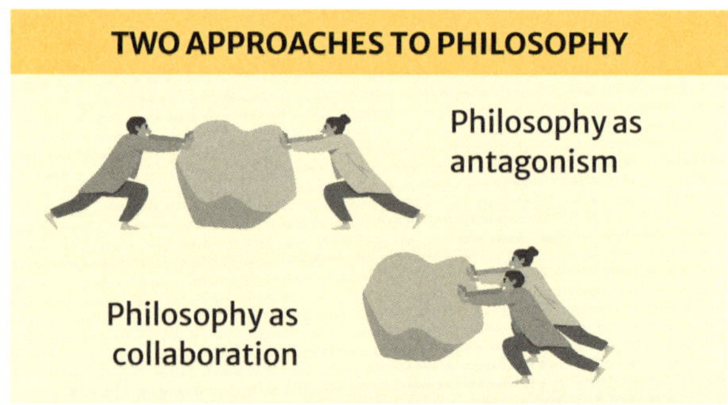

Dialectic and Philosophy

This Platonic model of investigating the truth often goes under the name of "dialectic." On the face of it, this means little more than discussion, but as practiced by Socrates this simple tool revealed profound truths of philosophy in many fields. The practice of philosophy as dialectic presupposes several things: 1) the fact that there is truth of some kind which can be found by the method of dialectic; 2) the earnest pursuit of truth by both parties, willing to put aside personal interests; 3) the discovery of philosophical truth is somehow more likely or only facilitated by pursuing it with at least another person.

CONDITIONS FOR DIALECTIC PHILOSOPHY

- **Some truths can only be found through discussion.**
- **Both sides must pursue truth, not self.**
- **Truth is easier to find in cooperation.**

Elenchus as a Test and Refutation

Now that we have established the context in which Socrates pursued his philosophical questions, we can move on to his elenchus—the sense that something that is being "tested" can fail the test, that it comes to be "refuted." As something that can be construed as a method, it is this elenchus that Socrates deploys on his interlocutors. Within the greater context of investigating and pursuing the truth through philosophical conversations the elenchus is not a personal attack to belittle or show the interlocutor up as a fool. It is a search for truth.

Testing for Consistency

The elenchus usually works by Socrates talking to someone and eventually two separate convictions are espoused by the interlocutor. These two separate convictions, by all appearances, are innocent enough, both to Socrates' interlocutor and even us as the reading audience. But soon Socrates turns this on its head. What he does is show that these two convictions, which we can call A and B, cannot be held by the same person. If one were to hold to conviction A, this would result in the denial of B. One conviction you might hold is that all crimes should be punished. We will call this A. Furthermore, after some discussion it turns out you hold that no one should be punished if the wrongdoing was done by the wrongdoer unwillingly, without his wanting to perform the wrongdoing. This we will call B.

So it turns out that there are some instances where you would grant that someone committed a wrongdoing unwillingly and you believe these circumstances excuse their crime in some way. Yet, simultaneously, you still hold to A, that *all* wrongdoing requires punishment, and B, that there

ELENCHUS SETUP

is an exception to all wrongdoing requiring punishment, in the case where the offender committed it unwillingly.

From the elenchus you will have to give up one of your convictions; you cannot hold to them both because one contradicts the other. It is perfectly reasonable to alter your view to something like, "Crimes should always be punished except in the case where the wrongdoer didn't know any better." The reason, among others, is that Socrates was encouraging people to think clearly by speaking consistently. He would be all too happy for you to nuance your view by making exceptions, as long as you were clear to state this. The process of the elenchus cannot go forward unless the beliefs of the discussants are out on the table.

In an interesting example of this process, Socrates tells Polus in the *Gorgias* dialogue that what he has said so far requires him to commit to the idea that *doing something wrong* is worse than *suffering wrong* at the hands of someone else.

"I think that I and you and all other men think committing evil is worse than suffering evil and not to be brought to justice is worse than being brought to justice." And Polus answered, "But I do not think that I nor any other human thinks this."

Gorgias, 474b6–11

In this exchange what we see clearly is that Socrates has gotten Polus to admit what his opinion is on a specific question, whether committing or suffering evil is worse. As it so happens, Polus says that suffering evil is worse, and it is this position that Socrates scrutinizes through the elenchus. A few pages later Polus, pressed for clarification, does admit that it is worse to do evil than to suffer it. But this would not have been possible had Polus not expressed his initial position clearly for Socrates to examine, challenge, and push him on it.

Elenchus as Process

Since there is a give and take to a dialogue by definition, the procedure may take a while, as a prolonged conversation is needed to establish agreement, disagreement, refutation, alteration of belief, and so forth. There is some truth to the idea that this could go on forever, and in a way this is at the heart of the philosophical life as Plato and Socrates both envision it—philosophy as a series of dialectical conversations, constantly taking up where it just left off in order to make progress.

The Elenchus is Personal

Plato depicts Socrates not as engaging the opinions of the reader, but that of his interlocutor. For the elenchus to work, it depends on, and only on, the person who is being tested agreeing that he does hold to the two convictions in question. No one else's opinions are relevant. It does not seem possible or even advisable to attempt an elenchus on more than a handful of people at one time. When you have more than the two opinions, there can be little headway, or possibility of agreement on even minor issues.

The personal nature of the elenchus also means that something is at stake for Socrates' interlocutor. For this reason Socrates asks his discussion partners to speak their minds, meaning that they share what they really believe and not what another might believe or what seems reasonable. In the dialogue *Protagoras* the character Protagoras wants to go along with what is said, without committing to anything. Socrates will have none of this.

What Socrates wants is to hear the earnest conviction of his interlocutor, not someone else's view, or a belief contrived simply for the sake of the conversation.

"I have no need of this 'if you wish' or an 'if it seems good to you,' to conduct an elenchus, but I have need of 'me and you.' And I say this 'me and you' because I think in this way the account is best put to the elenchus if someone gets rid of the hypothetical 'if.'"

Protagoras, 331c6–d1

The Results of the Elenchus

So far, the method demonstrates there is an inconsistency in the belief of the interlocutor, but it does not prescribe exactly where to go from there. There are several options. One is for Socrates' interlocutor simply to drop one of the convictions, either A or B. A second possibility is that one of either A or B or both is modified. In this change it may be that the explicit contradiction in the two beliefs is reconciled. Another somewhat humorous result is that the interlocutor is frustrated, angry, or retaliatory because his views were shown up in some way.

POSSIBLE RESULTS OF AN ELENCHUS

Action	Result
Drop either Belief A or Belief B	Consistency
Modify Belief A and/or Belief B	Modification
Drop Belief A and Belief B	Impasse

Socrates' dogged persistence in testing out the consistency of his fellow speakers earned him the reputation of being a gadfly, a large fly which goes

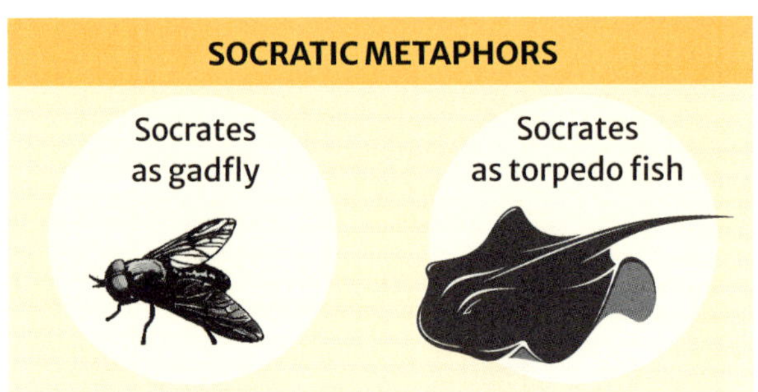

around stinging one cow and then the next. In the *Meno* dialogue Meno calls Socrates a torpedo fish, an animal which uses electrical charges to numb people. Socrates' retort is that he is himself numbed and if others are numbed, it is only because he is himself already numbed.

Aporia and Elenchus

Another option is that the elenchus has called both A and B into question and there is an impasse. A case can be made for preferring A over B and B over A, without a clear winner. In fact, some Platonic dialogues are called "aporetic." The word signifies that there is "no way or path." So the result we see in the dialogues with elenchus is sometimes no progress at all—remember, we are aiming at uncovering the truth in some single area of investigation. But this is no guarantee that the truth will be discovered. The very possibility of a stalemate, with no clear answer delivered, tells us something of the nature of philosophy in Plato's conception. Many have pointed out that this almost veers into a kind of skepticism, since we are not guaranteed any answers. The emphasis is on journey over destination. But keep in mind that Plato and Socrates are so persistent in their pursuit of the truth that it is very reasonable to suppose they were convinced the truth is out there, even though it is difficult to acquire.

Truth Over Personal Benefit

The difficulty of uncovering truth and acquiring knowledge can be found throughout the dialogues. This is one reason why philosophy turns out to be a "team sport" with multiple disputants trying to work through a problem together. When it comes to philosophy, we need all the help we can get. The *Gorgias* quotation with which we began the chapter gives us another key insight into the communal aspect of dialectic. Without a doubt there is an increase in intellectual horsepower when we engage in the preferred Platonic method of practicing philosophy together. But this is not the only reason, and perhaps not even the best reason to do so. As Socrates tells us, it does not matter whether he refutes or is refuted. To put it another way, it does not matter who has the truth, or the better approach to uncovering it. This is the implicit endorsement behind the dialectical approach: since we are all after the truth, but do not yet possess it, we need to go after it with every possible weapon we can find. Sometimes it is my idea, sometimes it is yours, sometimes it is some other person's. The spirit behind dialectical philosophy is it does not matter, because what we are after is ultimately beyond ourselves.

The Difficulty of Pursuing Truth

Despite the rather disinterested portrayal of dialectic and philosophy I have given of Socrates, in the encounters he had, things did not necessarily go so smoothly. One of the reasons is that whatever we think of Socrates' true motivations, without a doubt at least some of his interlocutors did not share his more noble aspirations. Just as in our own lives today, people in the Athens of Socrates' day had their own ideas and agendas, not to mention personal egos to manage. This means that very often Socrates would end up offending people with his method of testing and refutation. People generally *do* care that they are shown to be wrong. To be so preoccupied in acquiring the truth that your own pride is cast aside is very difficult to do.

The Stakes of Refutation

There are many things to fight over, Socrates could easily remind us, but there are few things actually worth fighting over. This is why in most of the Platonic dialogues Socrates is pursuing the truth concerning an ethical matter, such as the nature of piety or courage or justice. These are not mere quibbles about a game of chess or who forgot to close the refrigerator but about the timeless pursuit of ideas which still concern us today, on how to live and what the nature of reality is. These are worth putting aside our personal egos over.

Chapter 5

SOUL

Socrates: "To which class, of invisible or visible things, do we say the soul is more alike and natural to?"

Cebes: "It can't be seen by humans, at least."

Phaedo, 79b1–2

Plato tells us much about the soul throughout his dialogues. In the *Republic* he gives us arguments for why we should think there are three parts to it. In the *Phaedo* he gives us arguments for its immortality. In *Phaedrus* and *Symposium* he gives us even more insight into its nature and psychology. These are the more famous discourses on the soul in Plato, but the soul is seldom absent in any of his dialogues.

The Soul's Nature

What is the soul? If we take our cues from *Phaedo*, we find that it is some invisible thing existing in a mysterious interrelationship with the body. Most importantly the soul is divine and immortal, and this contrasts with the body, which is earthly and mortal. The soul too is the locus of all our mental content, our thoughts, emotions, desires, fears, and so forth. This is a sufficient sketch of the basics of the soul to get us started.

The nature of the soul is tied to our personal identity and to our view of the human body.

Tri-partite Soul

In the *Republic*, the soul serves a very important but unusual role, because a large part of the dialogue is an attempt to understand the soul by looking at the city. The idea is that looking to the city itself will give us an insight into how the soul is structured. The city is structured into three parts, and the soul also has this three-fold structure. The three parts are the logical, the spirited and the appetitive.

Each of these parts have their own drives and their own purpose. The ultimate aim, again mirroring that of the city, is to have each part in harmony with the others, performing its assigned role for its own benefit and the good of the whole soul.

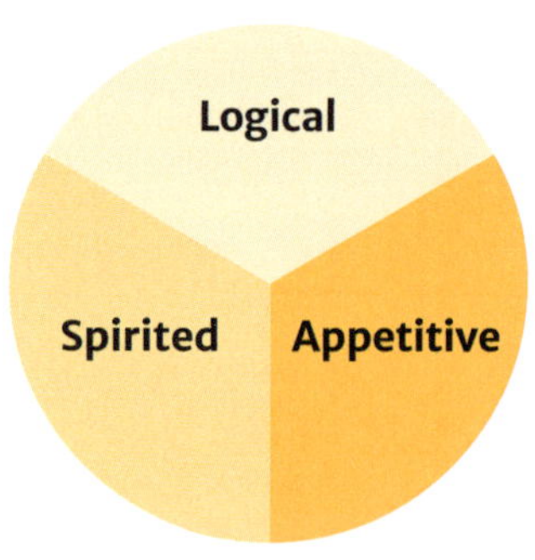

The Desires of the Tri-partite Soul

The logical concerns the rational aspects of the soul. This part of the soul reasons and deliberates, has insights and inferences. It should be no surprise that it is this part of the soul that is the most important. It is this part of the soul that not only desires knowledge, but seeks to rule the other parts of the soul. The spirited part of the soul is the part of the soul that seeks honor and esteem but is also the seat of anger and pride. At least in the *Republic* this part of the soul is not described in detail, so comparatively speaking its role is less clear than the others. Lastly we have the appetitive part of the soul.

TRI-PARTITE SOUL

Part of the Soul	Domain	Relationship to other parts of the soul
Logical	Knowledge/rule	Ruler
Spirited	Honor, passions	Helper of logical part
Appetitive	Physical and sexual appetites	Subordinate to logical and spirited parts

As its name implies this is the part of the soul in which the appetites live. Plato has in mind our appetite for food and sex primarily and perhaps exclusively.

The Ordering of the Soul

All three parts joined together account for the entirety of the human soul and, when harmonized, create a virtuous soul. In sketch this means that the intellective part of the soul rules over the whole soul and its two subordinate parts, but just as significantly, the spirited part serves as a second in command to help subdue the darker impulses of the appetitive soul. In a disordered soul the spirited and appetitive souls rebel against the intellective soul. Even worse is when the appetitive part by itself rules the soul. In addition to the relationships among the soul there is also the body, over which the soul is set like a guardian and source of life. To serve the body is to become a slave to pleasure, so it is important that the soul rules over the body to best see to the benefit of the whole person. The relationship of the soul to the body is of great weight in Plato.

"All soul cares for that which does not have a soul, and all soul goes around the heavens, at one time taking on some shapes and at other times other shapes."

Phaedrus, 246b7–10

The soul rules over everything inanimate, in the sense of conferring motion and life, but also by arranging and ordering the inanimate within the universe.

Soul and Body

Throughout Plato's dialogues there are a number of arguments for the immortality of the soul. This is an indication of the importance of immortality, but also of the soul itself, since the soul is set off against the body, which is described as mortal and crude. The body is like an anchor, not only fastening the soul to the cares of the body, but even after death this unhappy attachment to the body can hinder the soul from reaching the state of pure blessedness.

THE BODY IS AN ANCHOR

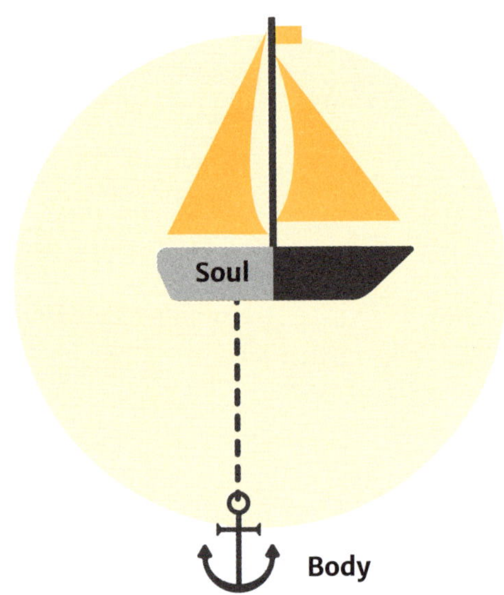

One very famous idea found in the dialogue *Phaedo* is the statement by Socrates that philosophy is nothing other than learning to die. The general idea is that the body is a confusing intruder upon the soul. We are constantly needing to attend to one need of our body or another, and furthermore the constant bombardment of our physical senses by stimuli takes us away from the pure, philosophical modes of contemplation. So philosophy is like dying in the sense that in death the soul experiences separation from the body. It is this separation from the body that the philosopher practices before death, deadening any reliance on the body.

To neglect the soul's independence from the body is to cultivate a slavish reliance of the soul on the body. Socrates poetically sums it up:

"Each pleasure and pain since it possesses, so to speak, a nail, nails the soul to the body and pins the soul and makes it bodily, and the soul thinks pleasure and pain are truth, and whatever else the body tells it are true. From sharing the same beliefs as the body and being forced to rejoice in these types of things I think it comes to share in the same habits and same diet as the body. It is never able to enter in Hades in purified state."

Phaedo, 83d2-9

Since immortality is the natural aim of the soul, it is important that we know we have a soul and what its basic nature is. In *Phaedo* there are four arguments for the immortality of the soul, which are of varying degrees of complexity. The traditional names for these are: the Argument from Opposites, the Argument from Recollection, the Affinity Argument, and the Final Argument. We will focus only on the Argument from Recollection, as it is fairly clear, yet ingenious, even if it is not persuasive. In other words, the creatively clever manner in which Plato sets the argument out will give us some of the best insight into the way his mind works.

The Argument from Recollection

This argument begins very humbly. It asks us to think about the relationship between *knowledge* and *remembering*. Is it possible to remember something you have not known beforehand? The answer appears to be no. I cannot remember my cat, Felix, unless I have first known about my cat, Felix. I cannot remember the play *Hamlet* unless I first knew what it was, and I cannot remember I left my

Is it possible to remember a cat without knowing it?

keys in the car unless I knew beforehand what my keys were. This interesting feature of how we recall, where remembering presupposes knowledge, will be important throughout the argument.

The next step is to acknowledge that all different kinds of things can spur us to remember. Obviously seeing a puppy can remind you of a puppy you used to own. But a puppy can also remind you of a person, because you know Laura who recently bought a puppy.

Or a puppy can remind you of a summer camp, because that's the first time you saw the animal. There are almost an innumerable amount of different associations you could have made in your memory.

The above associations we make with memory

work by dissimilarity. The reason that Socrates raises this distinction is that the argument from recollection will not make use of memories from dissimilarity but from similarity.

In the case of similarity our perception works like this. Take the example of seeing someone who looks like your father. You could say, "He reminds me of my father." Even implicit in saying this is the fact that this man is not identical in looks to your father. In other words, even with the similarity of remembering your mind is also drawn to the differences. The man is an inch or two shorter, and his ears are the wrong shape, and the hair is too thin, to be precisely like your father. In these cases of remembrance by similarity we can make a couple of observations. A pair of things, at least, are being compared, and in the comparison there is a sameness and there is also a difference.

To understand the next step we have to delve slightly into the metaphysical entities Plato calls "Forms." However, for the argument's sake here we only need to make use of how the Forms enable us to acquire knowledge. In this sense we can, instead of referring to "Forms," refer to "concepts," in

An everyday item like a bundle of sticks can be an entry into the question of "equality."

the normal sense of that word, for the purpose of understanding the Argument from Recollection. Imagine you have a bundle of sticks before you. You take two such sticks out and ask, "Are they equal?" Yes, they are equal, you think. But Plato prods us to understand how this is so. How do you form this concept of the equal, and how do you apply it to the sticks?

His answer, through Socrates, is that this too is an instance of memory and that we are prompted to remember by the sticks themselves. If you recall, we distinguished between remembering of things that are similar and those that are dissimilar. This is a case of remembering what is similar, of being reminded by the physical sticks, right in front of you. They remind us of the concept of the equal. The sticks you see before you are not perfectly equal in length, size, and shape, nor really could any two sticks be, whichever you chose. So, these sticks, as equals, are similar to the concept of equality, but differ because they are not exactly like equality—just as the man you saw earlier was not exactly like your father but reminded you of him. But if we return to the relationship between knowing and remembering from earlier, it was shown that remembering always requires that we first know what it is that we are remembering. This leads to the next step.

Equality Remembered

We cannot encounter true equality, exact similitude, between two different sticks in this world. At some level of inspection or measurement it will become apparent that the two sticks are not equal, either in

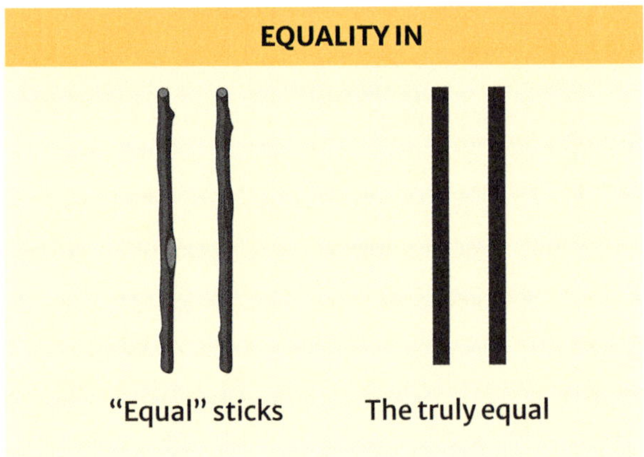

length, diameter, shape, quality, or whatever other parameter we want to compare them by.

These two sticks together remind us of equality, but that equality cannot be found anywhere on earth. No matter where we turn, every instance of equality we encounter in this earthly existence will fall short of the concept of equality.

Yet something mysterious is happening, even as we are limited by these earthly instances of equality. This is the fact that we even have an idea of equality with which the instances of equality can be compared. According to the argument as it has been explained, since the particular equal sticks reminded us of the idea of equality, this means we previously had knowledge of the idea of equality. But we have also conceded the point that since no earthly example of equality is exactly like the concept of the equal, we must have gotten the concept of equal somewhere besides this current earthly existence. It is here that Plato's Socrates suggests that this must have come before our birth, and this means we must have lived before, when we first became acquainted with that knowledge.

The soul's immortality is the most clear way Plato emphasized its importance. But it is also responsible for our reason and appetites, and is most aptly identified with our true selves. The soul is complex to understand, but this knowledge of the self is absolutely crucial to understanding the human animal.

Chapter 6

VIRTUE IS KNOWLEDGE

"No one who either knows or thinks other things are better than the things which he does, given they are possible to be done, than does the things which are less good when it is permissible to do the better things. To be beneath oneself is nothing other than ignorance, and mastering oneself is nothing other than wisdom."

Socrates, *Protagoras* 358c

Virtue—does it concern the mind, the actions only, or is it merely a matter of the will? These questions about virtue were of great concern to Plato, and in the Platonic dialogues Socrates spends a great deal of time investigating moral questions. Socrates as a philosopher has been conventionally understood as a man concerned with ethical inquiry, doggedly pursuing the answer to various definitions of "What is X?," where X is some ethical term such as "courage" or "piety."

The Origin of Ethics

The Greek word "ethics" arises from two complementary ideas. One is that "ethos" refers to the customary place of animals, i.e. wherever they happen to be found. This idea pairs nicely with the other formative meaning of ethics, which is that it concerns the habits and customs of someone. The idea of ethics then, is whatever you do regularly, your set of habits, where you "hang out" metaphorically.

ETHICS IS WHEREVER YOU SPEND YOUR TIME

In this broad descriptive sense the term "ethics" is neither good nor bad, as it only gives us the truth about how someone acts.

Virtue, surprisingly, is an ethically neutral term. It can apply to anything, just as the Greek word "virtue" translates as "aretē," means "excellence," and all kinds of things can be excellent without invoking the category of morality. But in the particular case of ethics we care about, excellence in moral virtue, it concerns living well, the good way to act.

Seeking the Good

Perhaps the most important philosophical assumption to understand the idea that virtue is knowledge is that seeking the good is the basic driver of human action. People seek what is good and shun what is bad. This does not imply that

people actually know what is good or bad, only that whatever they happen to think is good, they pursue such an apparent good. Even the professional thief, for example, conducts his robberies in such a way because he believes that in so doing this will be good for him.

Considering the case of someone who desires what is bad, Socrates rejects that possibility with this explanation.

"So then it is clear that those men do not desire bad things who are ignorant of them, but they desire those things which they think are evil, and these things, at any rate, turn out to be bad. So the result is that because they are ignorant of these evils and think they are good it is clear that they are desiring good things."

Meno, 77e1–4

Virtue and Knowledge

When it comes to Socrates and Plato, the relationship between virtue and knowledge is quite intimate. In fact, many have dubbed this approach to virtue as "Socratic intellectualism," because of their insepara-bility. In a nutshell the idea is quite simple. To know the good is to choose that good thing. To not choose the good thing means that you do not understand what the good is—for you would have chosen the good had you understood that it was good.

SOCRATIC INTELLECTUALISM

Knowing the good → **Choosing the good**

Ignorance of the good → **Choosing the bad**

This is a broadly applicable psychological principle, but it is of particular importance when it comes to ethical issues. Although this is the heart of the idea, there is still more to be said about the claim that virtue is knowledge.

The context for the quotation opposite has in mind actions of one kind or another. What kind of actions ought we to perform, good ones or bad ones? The Platonic contention is that if there is some set of options, where one action is good or best, and the others fall short in some way, we will always pick that best, noble course of action, provided we know that it is the best. In other words, ignorance is the enemy of the good. If we have the wrong notion about what to choose, then, and only then, do we choose what is not good. If virtue is knowledge, vice is ignorance.

Weakness of Will

This understanding of virtue does not allow for a situation in which you have a weakness of the will. For example, if you are on a diet and eat a number of chocolate chip cookies, the Platonic explanation will not be that your will caved in. The diagnosis for your slippage will be that you did not really know the cookies would be harmful to your diet. In this example, this is perhaps difficult to swallow. Surely, someone who has had any experience with a diet knows that there are frequent and regular failures to keep to the diet. So how can one claim there is an ignorance of the outcome? Well, this is exactly what is being claimed.

Virtue as Knowledge Defended

The idea that whenever we err we do so due to a lack of understanding can be defended in several ways. The first is to consider that when people choose one course of action over another it is because they are choosing what seems good. Even in the case of a man who eats cookies for breakfast, we can suppose that he thinks this choice appears better than others.

Another reason to think that virtue is knowledge is that a merely casual acceptance of something might not count as knowledge. That is, even if we accept loosely the proposition, "cookies make us gain weight and feel poorly," we must still make the necessary step of connecting that to our current circumstances. The acknowledgement of responsibility, in other words, is the type of knowledge we need to possess in order for the ethical lesson to take. Another point is that we need to have a holistic account of the reasons and options available to us to say we have knowledge. Some people, in fact, eat cookies for their diet, grow out of shape and despondent, and they even know that this lifestyle leads to being obese and despondent. But perhaps what they do not know is that there is a different way to live and to eat, and relatedly, how to manage that lifestyle by proper grocery purchases and cooking habits. If only they could be introduced to this knowledge, then comparatively the choice to stick with cookies would appear as it is—an inferior and unwelcome activity. A last reason to think that virtue is knowledge has some credence to it is that very often destructive activities have some lag. It can be difficult for people to imagine that their choices now will only come home to roost much later on. If they could experience bad results instantaneously, then they would not choose many of the things they do. Upon examination what we can say about this contention that "virtue is knowledge," is that it is not as wild an idea as it first appears. There are reasons we can marshal to its support.

The Power of Knowledge

It is an oft repeated slogan that "Knowledge is power." In Plato this takes on a distinct meaning, as knowledge really possesses power in a distinct way. Since humans are naturally oriented to desire the good and pursue the good when it has been revealed to them, this means that knowledge can overtake anything. If there is a temptation to do something bad, having knowledge of the good will destroy this temptation. As a choice, good will always beat what is bad. In this sense, good is unconquerable. In the case of addiction, this would look something like an epiphany in a case where a drug addiction is overcome. There comes a moment when the addict sees the addiction for what it is, as some kind of evil compared to a life without the drug. As soon as the drug-free life is seen as the good, this is the beginning of the addict's path to recovery.

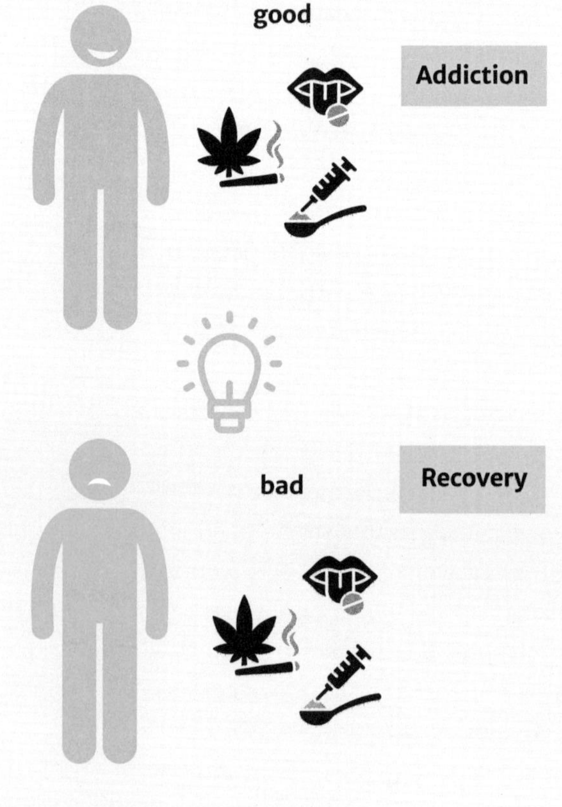
OVERCOMING ADDICTION AS INTELLECTUAL INSIGHT
good
Addiction
bad
Recovery

The Appeal of Socratic Intellectualism

What exactly is at stake for Plato and Socrates in wishing to promote and defend this idea? One benefit is that it simplifies ethical life. All you have to do is find out what the best thing is in a given situation or more generally, how to lead a good life, and you will do it. On the other hand this puts an exclusive premium on the attainment of knowledge. Investigating and learning suddenly take on a supreme importance if virtue is nothing more than knowing what is good. Even though this simplifies the process of ethics, this does not mean it is easy to do the right thing by knowing the right thing. But one thing it does highlight is that removing the veil from the good is sufficient on its own to entice us to pursue the good. Ignorance of the good forms shackles binding us, while knowledge of the good has a necessary force in compelling us toward it.

Real and Apparent Good

On Plato's account there are a multitude of apparent goods out there so that our recognition of the good is far from guaranteed. Sometimes something appears

Deliberation for the sage is important because the good is

good because it is good, but sometimes it appears good because someone is trying to deceive you that it is good, such as a politician persuading you of a new policy, or a con man trying to swindle you out of your money with a product that turns out to be a hunk of junk. Knowledge is difficult to acquire because there are a lot of imposters and frauds. So goodness has a two-fold importance when it comes to Platonic psychology. On the one hand, whatever we view as the good we will pursue. On the other, we do not want to pursue just whatever we happen to think is good. There needs to be great labor in pursuit of knowledge so that we can have assurance that what we pursue is a real not apparent good. Only when we have the true good in view is it worth pursuing.

The Self and Virtue

There is one more element to this theory of knowledge. This is the idea that as important as knowledge of the external world is, it is even more vital to understand the self. The importance of self-knowledge is a persistent theme in the Socratic pursuit of knowledge, and it is not hard to see why. If we are ignorant of our own nature, then we are missing crucial information which affects how we think and act. And since virtue, whatever else it concerns, is primarily about our individual actions, it stands to reason that we need to have an understanding of ourselves as individuals in order to make the kind of informed decisions we think virtue as knowledge demands.

At any rate, this knowledge of the self, besides a general mood of reflection about what we are and do, also demands that we know the parts of the soul and how this affects our life as a whole person. This includes knowing the three parts of the soul, their interactions, and especially their desires, and how they best work together. To be virtuous you have to have a well-ordered soul, and for the soul to be well ordered is to have knowledge: knowledge of what is good for the soul and what is good generally—goods which when known are necessarily pursued.

The desired state of the ordered condition of the soul, where the intellectual part of the soul, with the help of the spirited, subdues and controls the appetitive, also parallels the importance of knowledge in the soul for the attainment of virtue.

Once the soul, as a duly ordered whole, knows this order and submits itself to this best arrangement, then this is the preliminary condition making all further knowledge possible. The soul so ordered has set the stage to find out what is good and true in all other areas of inquiry.

Chapter 7

FORMS

"I think that you think that each Form is one is from the following consideration. Whenever you think some many things are large, you think there is perhaps one idea, the same one, as you look at them, from which you think the 'Large' is one thing."

Parmenides 132a, 1–2

Plato's theory of Forms, or Ideas, is familiar to most people as a vague concept. But as with much of Plato, it exists as a caricature, and not through any intentional misrepresentation. Forms are a forceful theme in the dialogues, with obvious significance and there are admittedly difficult descriptions of how we are to conceive of these entities known as "Forms."

In brief, a Form is that which accounts for both how we humans can come to know something as well as how that thing comes to exist. If we take an orange tabby, a calico, a Maine Coon, and a Siamese cat, we see that all of these belong to the category and idea of "cat." But how do we come to know something that we call "cat," which all examples of cat fall under? And how is it that although all these cats differ between themselves and each of which is not a perfect specimen of a cat, yet our single idea of Cat is both perfect and determines how each cat is a cat? These are the kind of questions Plato was interested in answering as he came up with his theory of Forms.

Etymology of Forms

The most common word that Plato uses to describe a Form is "eidos." This word principally refers to the visible shape an object takes. But Plato applies the idea of "shape" as a kind of metaphor, to refer to what we would call the "structure" of something. The main reason this gets transformed into a metaphor is that Forms are something invisible. Consequently there is no actual shape or form, but only figuratively can there be said to be a "Form." But as we will see, this is not to be understood as claiming that Forms are only imaginary or that they are derivative.

The Really Real

For Plato the Forms are not only real, but more real than what we see before us in the physical world. This is because everything in the physical world is dependent on the world of Forms. But it is also true that the Forms are unlike physical things in that they do not change, unlike the wilting rose, the ever shifting river and the aging beauty queen.

This means that Forms are both like things we see around us, but they are also substantially unlike them, in that the Forms are better and more real.

From a broad perspective Plato's theory of Forms involves how things in this world are different, the same, and similar to the world of Forms. In this and the next chapter we will flesh this out even more, but here it will be enough to point out that the theory's complexity means that we have many different aspects to consider.

Knowing and Being

What is the theory of Forms about? It is about both how we come to know things but also how things are on their own independently of how we know them. Knowing and being are on their own two large areas of philosophy, the study of the intimidating sounding "epistemology" and "ontology" respectively, but in Plato's thinking they are linked and inseparable. This will result in some surprising conclusions about the Forms.

Starting with Forms

The quotation from the *Parmenides* dialogue on page 109 is a good starting point for Forms. The reason is that it straightforwardly gives us the perspective of someone, perhaps even Plato himself, coming to appreciate the idea of Forms. In this particular example it is "largeness" in question, but take "beautiful," or "equal" or any of a multitude of terms. The point is that we see particular things that are different, say a group of dogs, but they are also united in a similar way by something over and above their particularity as different dogs.

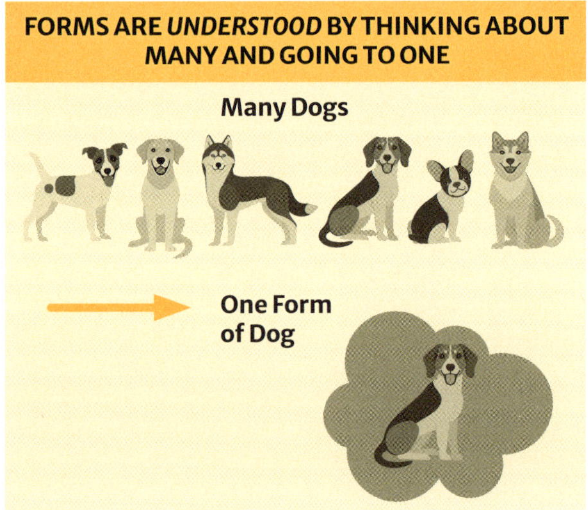

Particulars and Forms

One way to consider the physical things that are not Forms is to refer to them as particulars. They have this name because they are "particular" instances of the universal Form. A particular beautiful thing stands in a relation to the Form of Beauty. The particular stands in a subordinate relationship to the Form itself. This means that it is different, but also that it is inferior. Nevertheless, as we will see, these particulars have a necessary role in our coming to understand the Forms. Without them we would not come to know the Forms as we do.

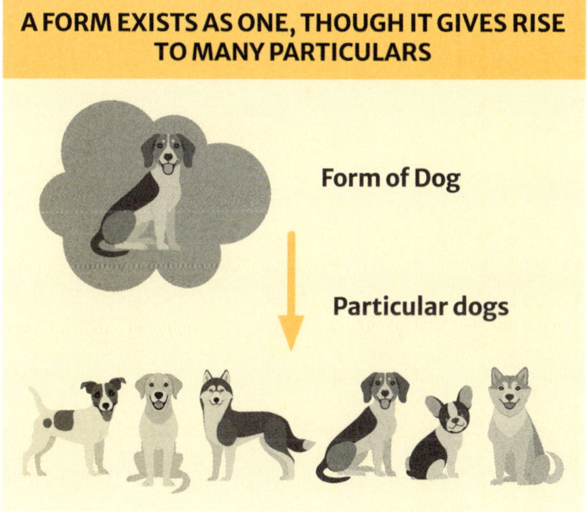

In the *Phaedo* we read how the Form of something, as contrasted with the particular, does not change.

"This nature itself [i.e. The Form], which we are trying to give an account of the way it is by asking and answering—is it always the same way according to the same things or is it one way at one time and a different way at another time? The equal itself, the beautiful itself, and each thing itself which it is, being as it is—will they not ever undergo any kind of change whatsoever?"

Phaedo, 78d1–9

Particulars into Forms

Imagine we are driving through a wealthy neighborhood and see a number of mansions lining the streets. We acknowledge these houses are "large." But how does this come about? While evidently the houses are distinct from each other, there is some common element which we designate as their "largeness." But in so seeing, we do not think that this largeness belongs properly to any one of them. It is only as a group that their largeness, so to speak, comes out. But on deliberation what we further come to realize is that the important "grouping" of the houses is not what is happening before our eyes but in our minds. We can group things that are not near each other and it is only in the inner eye of the mind that the common element, in this case their largeness, is seen and understood. This is a reasonable basic explanation of the way in which we come to know a Form, by a mental comparison with many examples.

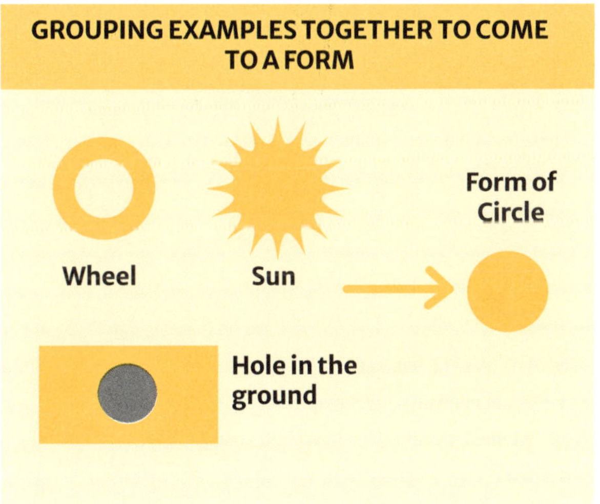

Plato developed the idea of Forms, a controversial and influential contribution to philosophy.

This is a common explanation that could be equally accepted by different philosophers, psychologists, and neuroscientists for the mental phenomenon that Plato referred to as Forms. What sets Plato apart, and into controversial territory, is his insistence that Forms have an existence entirely independent of the mind.

Forms as Paradigms

A Form is a paradigm for Plato. This means that it serves as a model for earthly instances of that same thing. Being a model means that it is perfect and uniquely perfect—everything that comes after it is but a copy. There is only a single Form of Beauty, for example, and it is this Form of Beauty from which all instances of beauty take their own individual beauty. Plato's technical word for the relationship between a particular thing and the Forms it is named after is "participation." The beautiful woman participates in the Form of Beauty and the large house participates in the Form of Large. Why does Plato employ this hedging language? This is an acknowledgement that the things in this world are imperfect and constantly changing. So the beautiful woman does not stay beautiful, she changes through time, unlike the Form of Beauty which is unchangeably beautiful. She is said to only "participate" because her partaking of Beauty is only provisional—there is nothing that requires her to always remain beautiful, as is the case with the Form of Beauty. The beautiful woman gets hold of beauty only temporarily and partially, so she "participates" in Beauty for a season, and then it passes beyond her.

The Form of Beauty exceeds the beauty of the most beautiful woman.

Beauty is Beautiful

Along with the fact that Forms are paradigms there is another equally important, but admittedly odd, feature. The Form of Beauty is itself beautiful. The Form of Justice is itself just. The Form of Equal is itself equal. The thinking behind this is that if the Form of Beauty is not beautiful then it will not be able to confer this beauty to anything else. A Form cannot give what it does not possess.

Forms are Distinct

As has ben discussed, Forms are perfect while particular instances are not. This distinction brings up the divide that exists between Forms and those things that merely participate in them. Things in this world are visible, palpable, earthly, and changing. In fact it is the physical nature of these particulars which probably explains why they are always shifting daily into one kind of change or another. The Forms, on the other hand, are immutable, invisible, untouchable, divine and so unchanging. So while there is a relationship between Form and particular, this mysterious participation, the Forms could very well be said to be more different than they are the same. This is one reason why the Forms are said to dwell in a "heavenly realm." Because they are so different from the earthly realm, they could not possibly dwell here. Everything as we experience it in the physical domain changes or is corrupted in some way. Forms stabilize, as it were, the physical world. It is not only the case that particular physical instances only derivatively possess a property that the Form itself possesses outright, but also these particulars would not exist in any way, shadowy impersonations as they are, without the Forms.

More of the Forms on Knowing

But Forms account for not only how things are, but how we humans come to understand anything at all. If we return again to the opening quotation, note that it concerns how we come to discern different aspects of things. Earlier we discussed the motivation for why Plato thought Forms were a good explanation for how we understand a single property belonging to many instances, say of largeness. But, in fact, Plato's Theory of Forms is much more expansive than this. Forms account for everything we see and understand. We see a group of large things. We say that each one of them is large, even though each one might have a different color and be a different type of object: a large pot, a large dog, a large house, a large shoe. There is only one Form of Largeness and one Form of Dog, as Plato only grants there is one Form for each type of thing. The particular large dog, Fido, participates in both the Form of Dog and the Form of Large.

PARTICIPATION IN A FORM

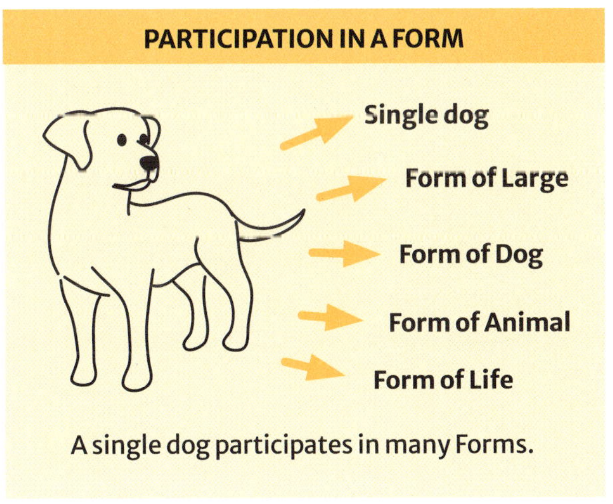

A single dog participates in many Forms.

But no less fantastically, at least from our perspective, the owner, Tim, comes to know his dog, Fido, by coming to know the Form of Dog and Form of Large, and any other Forms Fido happens to participate in.

Even though we can see things that are large, it is important to remember that a Form itself cannot be seen. So although we can come to recognize a Form by the help of examples, those examples are not themselves the Form. A large horse or a large rock are not the Form of Largeness. Socrates puts it this way in *Phaedo*:

"By any bodily perception have you grasped the Forms? I mean all of them, for example, have you grasped the Form of Largeness or Health or Strength, or the essence of each of the other Forms, whichever essence they happen to have?"

Phaedo 65d7–11

In Plato there is a happy concord between what a thing is and how we come to know it. This is one of the appealing aspects of Plato, as his thinking locks together in a consistent whole, even if we think that some of his theorizing tends to the wild side. In the Forms, what we see is an account of the mind and the world that the mind interacts with, an attempt to explain how a universal description such as "beauty" or "animal" is shared among different things, and a reconciliation of the changing nature of the world with our mental understanding. Its most significant liability for some will count as its greatest asset for others. As soon as we admit Forms into our world, we have granted the interruption of an entirely foreign realm. That world or realm is something radically different than what our physical world is like. In turn, this raises questions about the interaction between our world and the world of Forms. This will concern the next chapter.

Chapter 8

TWO WORLDS

"Keep in mind, just as we were saying, there are two rulers, and one rules the intelligible kind and place, the other kind I refer to as visible... So then you have these two kinds, visible and intelligible."

Republic, 509d

In the last chapter on Forms we saw that our knowledge of a thing matches up with how that thing really is. That is, knowledge resembles or parallels whatever it is about. This recognition that the ways things are influences how we come to understand them will be crucial in our understanding of two worlds in this chapter.

From the previous chapter on Forms we already have seen there is a division between Forms and the particulars which participate in those Forms. But there is another way that the universe is divided into two. By Plato's time there was a dispute about the nature of the world. Is the world always the same and singular, or is the world always changing and multifold? Plato's Two World theory is in some ways an attempt to reconcile these two viewpoints. Change is something essentially involved with this visible universe while the world of the unchanging Forms requires unchanging permanence. Coming to understand these two worlds will call for a different mode of comprehension for each. If we can trace Plato's motivation for introducing his Two World theory it would center on the way in which we can have any knowledge of things that are always changing. Plato's shocking answer is that you cannot.

The Divided Line

In Plato, the relationship of Forms and particulars is developed much further than what we saw in the last chapter. In exploring this we will look at what has come to be described as Plato's Divided Line from the sixth book of the *Republic*. The first move is perhaps the most controversial, for it divides everything into what we might term the "material" (or physical) and "immaterial." Now, this might seem unremarkable, but Plato does not just mean to designate numbers or the laws of logic as in the immaterial realm. Or rather he is not content with them alone, admittedly immaterial as they are. Further, the designation "immaterial" is not just a nice complement to "material." What is immaterial is manifestly superior to what is not. All else we learn about Plato and his two worlds must first begin with acknowledging that the immaterial is not merely different, but better, than the material.

Two Worlds

Visible	Intelligible
Material World	Immaterial World
Realm of particulars	Realm of Forms
Inferior	Superior
Tangible	Intangible
Changing	Changeless

In Plato's words (as seen in the quotation on page 127) the material is described as the "visible," while the immaterial is described as the "intelligible." The term "intelligible" captures the fact that it is grasped by the "intellect," the rational faculty of the soul. The "visible" draws our attention to the earthly sense organs which perceive the things of this physical world. Once again, even at this general level, we see that Plato closely associates what exists with how we know it.

The general difference between the intelligible realm and the visible realm is mirrored by the soul which discerns the intelligible realm and the physical senses which discern the visible realm. Socrates draws the distinction clearly by putting it this way:

"So then the soul reasons most wonderfully at those times when it is grieved by none of the following: the sense of hearing, nor sight, nor pain nor any pleasure, but as much as is possible the soul comes to be as much as possible by itself and having nothing to do with the body, and as much as it is able the soul shares nothing in common with the body not even desiring to touch it as it stretches out for true being."

Phaedo 65c3–8

Imagination

This is only the beginning of the divided line, however. Each of these divisions of intelligible and visible is divided once further. Let us begin in the visible realm. It is here that we find the lowest of all forms of "knowing"—a term we can use loosely but which properly will belong only to the single highest of the two kinds of intelligible beings. This lowest form of knowing is imagination. The Greek word for "imagination," phantasia, just as the Latin word which English "imagination" is derived from, centers on appearance and sight. This is because imagination concerns images. These apparent images come about when one thing in the physical world reflects off another thing in the physical world. Such would include reflections off of a mirror, or in water, or any shiny object at all. Also included are shadows, as a certain kind of reflection.

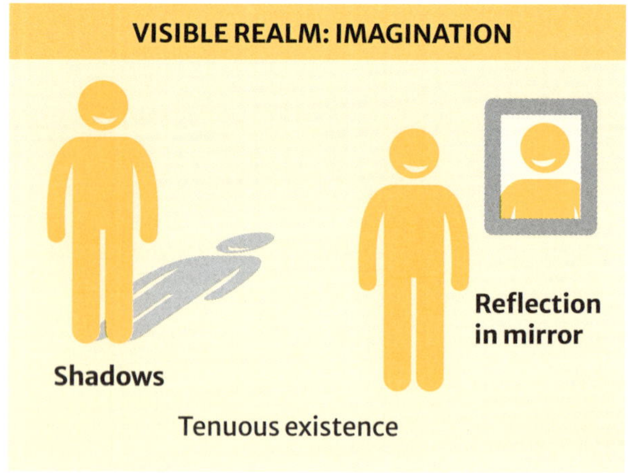

What these all have in common is that they are derivative, not of a higher level of reality, but of the everyday and common. The shadow is of a physical tree, and the reflection in the mirror is of a visible room. These types of ephemeral entities are entirely dependent on other things, and they copy them in only a partial, temporary and inferior way.

Belief

Accordingly, as you may have guessed, the next rung of the divided line is comprised of those things the shadows and reflections are shadows and reflections of. Plato says these objects belong to the realm of "belief." Imagination corresponds to what is seen, in the sense of merely appearing, whereas the things in the realm of belief are a step above this. They are not so insubstantial as to be mere reflections and shadows, but are the things that we typically conceive as populating our physical world: people, plants, animals and all the artifacts of the human hand. Accordingly we have a somewhat more secure grasp on what they are because they do not belong to imagination alone.

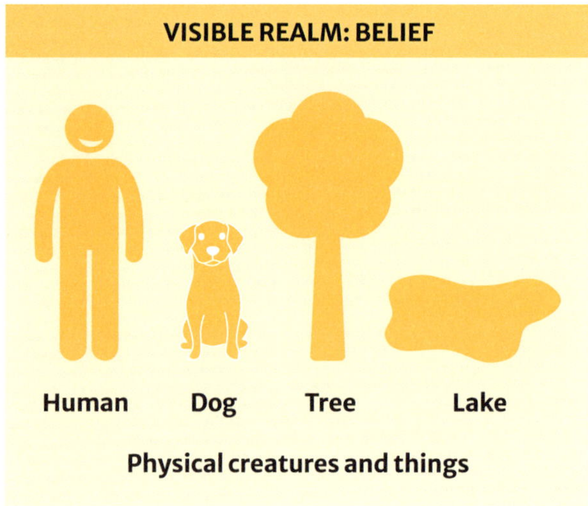

These two bottom divisions of the divided line are filled by images. Together they constitute the visible portion of reality. But there is still the other half of the divided line, what Plato terms the intelligible.

The Intelligible

In the intelligible realm we have "thought" and "understanding." Thought is kind of a mediator between the visible and intelligible realms because it makes use of what is visible as hypotheses. That is, certain things are presupposed as true in order to achieve a goal. Plato brings up the example of mathematical sciences which often make unproved assumptions in order to come to a truth. For example, mathematicians assume there are odd and even numbers and the sum of the interior angles of a triangle is 180 degrees. At this level there is still a level of accommodation to the visible. This is because it makes use of mathematical and geometrical figures, even though the real object of study and pursuit is not physical at all.

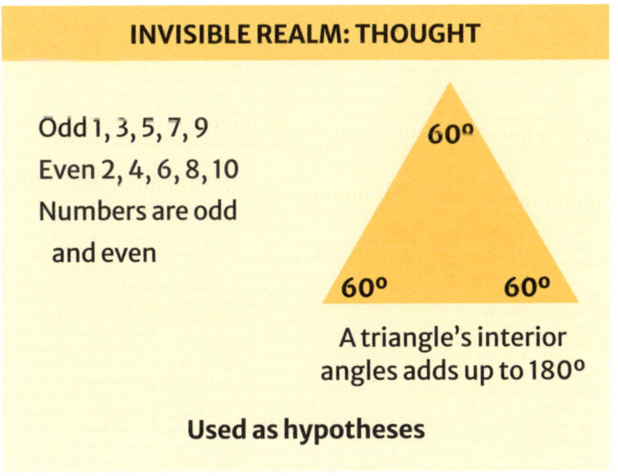

The geometrician is focused on the geometrical conception of the circle, not the drawn circle which will always fall short because its perimeter can never be depicted as equally and perfectly equidistant from the center of the figure as a true circle is.

So it turns out that even in this next-to-highest level of the divided line, we are still dependent on images. Just as imagination is an image for belief, so the objects that populate belief are used as images for thought. In other words, the level above uses the level below as an image, partly because it is a superior and more substantial reality and the level below it is less real.

Understanding

The higher section of the intelligible is that which belongs to understanding. This is the highest level and it alone is able to operate without the use of images. At this level the soul is able to make use of Forms alone to be able to reason. At this level Forms not only are what begins the process of reasoning, but this is where reason ends as well. What exactly this amounts to is difficult to determine, but what can be said is that in the case of understanding the knowledge gained is the most certain of all. This is one reason why Plato is careful to point out that understanding does not make use of unproven assumptions, but it operates by an entirely unhypothesized first principle.

We come to understanding through dialectic. Most often in the dialogues this term is used to refer to the method of reasoning through philosophical problems by two or more interlocutors. Here it probably involves something more, such as the purely conceptual conclusions that such a process involves, and that in practice may include only a single person "dialoguing" alone, in private contemplation.

At any rate, there are four sections of the divided line, each of which represents both a kind of being and a kind of knowing. What a thing is determines how it is conceived, and the manner in which we think in turn limits the kind of things that we are able to understand. The objects of imagination possess the least degree of reality, and consequently we can only "imagine" them, we cannot "understand" them. That is, their derivative existence is reflected

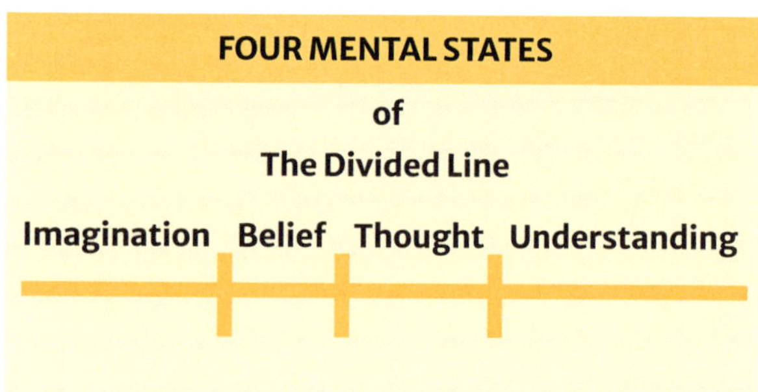

in the somewhat tenuous way we are able to grasp hold of them. A shadow, the nebulous and generic entity that it is, can never be discriminated by us with the detail that a person casting that shadow can be, for example. The shadows of two people look remarkably alike in contrast to the people themselves.

Forms and Particulars

In the previous chapter we have read about Forms. Now we can place the two primary elements we talked about there, Forms and their particulars, the individual instances which participate in the Forms, into the Two World theory. The Forms are the only proper objects that can be known. Knowing is only a power that can be directed to Forms, in much the same way that the ear can only be directed to sounds or the eye can only see things that are visible. The particulars, such as an individual man, Socrates, or an individual horse, Bucephalus, can only be believed in.

Understanding and Ignorance

Another approach to appreciating the distinctions that Plato draws between these different types of mental content is to consider understanding and ignorance. Understanding concerns "what is." It involves the Forms, which always are and always will be, unchanging and eternally being what they are. Ignorance concerns what is not, that which does not exist at all. In between understanding and ignorance is belief. As the middle state between understanding and ignorance, belief is set over things that both are and are not. What does it mean to both be and not be? The idea is that because the particular objects of this world are always in flux, they are never the same thing from moment to moment. They are continuously changing from one

Ancient Greek man and woman talking.

thing to the next, never quite going out of existence but never remaining the same either. Thus they are halfway between being and not-being.

The objects of belief can only be "believed," the objects of thought can only be "thought," and the objects of understanding can only be "understood." Again, the way we know something indicates the hierarchy of Plato's divided line. The more substantiality there is, the higher we go, and the higher both the quality and the certainty of the knowledge that accompanies that thing. Glaucon, Socrates' interlocutor at this point in the *Republic*, sums it up this way.

"And in these four sections four mental states occur in the soul. Understanding happens in the highest, thinking happens in the second highest, and in the third place is belief and last is imagination, and arrange these in a ratio so that each of these mental conditions partakes of the truth to the same degree it partakes of clarity."

Republic, 511d7–e5

At the highest point of mental contemplation is the Form of the Good. It is this Form that Plato says is "beyond being." It is the Form of the Good that accounts for the knowing of the things that are known and for the being of the things that exist. It too can be known, but beyond this Plato has not said more.

Chapter 9

GODS

"Therefore it is necessary to attempt to escape from here to there as quickly as possible. And escape from the world is becoming like to God as far as possible. And likeness is becoming just and holy with practical wisdom."

Theaetetus, 176a4–b2

In Plato, as in all of Greek literature, the gods are never far away, sometimes taking center stage but always lurking somewhere as important features of the cultural background. In talking about the gods there is the relationship which the people have with the gods, their religion and piety, but also their conception of the gods themselves. As in any religious discussion the existence of the gods has a bearing on how people act and what they believe to be most important in life and ultimately in the order of all things.

Socrates and Religion

Plato's cultural background certainly includes the assumption of polytheism, and it appears that this is never entirely rejected. Nevertheless, as we know from Socrates' trial, religious innovation was a dangerous enterprise in Ancient Athens. Socrates was accused of introducing strange new gods to the city as well as corrupting the youth, two charges which are interlinked. You also have the issue of Socrates' daimonion, a mysterious divine-like spirit which would appear to warn

Socrates when he was about to do something he should not. The influence of this daimonion could never be uncontroversial both because it offered moral guidance and functionally served as a source of religious authority.

These are just the main and generally known religious considerations we find in Plato and with Socrates. But though it does not garner a lot of attention, the theme of religion and the gods is extremely important in Plato. Even in the beginning of Plato's most famous work, *Republic*, Socrates is making his way to see the procession being conducted for the benefit of Bendis, a Thracian (note: foreign) goddess. At the end of what is arguably Plato's next most famous dialogue, *Phaedo*, Socrates dramatically meets death by drinking hemlock, but does not depart before asking his friends to offer a sacrificial cock to Asclepius, the god of healing. Even in the details of the dialogues the gods are lurking near.

The forced suicide of Socrates owed in part to his controversial view of the gods.

Likeness to the Gods

The quotation at the head of this chapter demonstrates the serious stakes of religious belief and practice for Plato. It is not the case that religion is something merely appended to how we act and believe. The context for the *Theaetetus* quotation concerns how and why we are to shun evil and pursue the good. This is not entirely possible in our earthly existence. But this is precisely why we ought to seek to imitate God as much as we are capable. This imitation in turn is not a call to transform our human form into some divine being, whatever that would look like. Rather it is a path of pursuing the virtues, among which are named justice, understanding, and piety. The mention of piety should pique our attention, since it sticks out as unique in contrast to the traditional four Greek virtues, held in common among Athenians: wisdom, temperance, justice, and courage. Piety, it turns out, is something much more capacious than we might think. It not only concerns a kind of disposition towards the gods but importantly it requires that we act as the gods themselves behave, as just, as wise, and brave and temperant.

The attempt to emulate the gods, though chiefly in thought and behavior, does not end there. In the *Republic* and in the later *Laws* Plato explicitly accords divine honors and treatment to men who have achieved greatness.

It is worth noting that Plato's depiction of the gods is not quite in keeping with Greek or even Athenian orthodoxy. That tradition, steeped in Homer, held that the gods fought with one another, committed adultery with themselves and humans, engaged in deceit of various kinds and other rather immoral behaviors.

Plato often objected to anthropomorphic depictions of the gods, though he too made use of them.

Plato did not tolerate this theology, and in fact expels its advocates, including the poets, from his ideal city in the *Republic* precisely because they encourage this impious talk about the gods.

Nevertheless, Plato apparently receives the tradition of the 12 traditional Olympic gods without any reservation of conscience. In the *Phaedrus*, in the central myth about the soul, he portrays Zeus at the head of the gods leading the rest of the divine company to gaze upon pure being. The description of Zeus and the gods is colorfully poetic, but keeping in line with the traditional understanding.

"Zeus, the great leader in heaven, drives a winged chariot, going first, arranging and taking care of everything. The army of the gods and daimons follow him arranged in eleven parts."

Phaedrus 246e4–247a1

In the *Symposium*, successive speakers take turns giving praise to the god of love.

When it comes to practice we see in Plato's dialogues much the same as we would expect in any religion. There are offerings and sacrifices to the gods. We also see prayer to the gods, often before a character makes a philosophically weighty speech, such as in the *Phaedrus* and in the cosmological speech in *Timaeus*.

In *Phaedrus*, Plato says that different human personalities take after a unique Greek god.

But perhaps the most significant relationship we have with the gods is their claim over us. In the *Crito* and *Phaedo* Socrates says that we are the property of the gods. He brings this up in the context of suicide, that we are not our own to do with as we please. The gods will grant us our fate in time, without any attempt on our own part to take it into our own hands. Here is Socrates' description of the relationship men have with the gods.

"We humans are in a certain prison and each person must certainly not escape or run away from this prison, and this appears to me as a wondrous account and not easy to see clearly. But it seems to me well said that the gods take care of us and that we humans are one of the possessions of the gods."

Phaedo 62b4–10

COSMIC SOULS

The universe has a soul

The stars have souls

The Number of the Gods

We have the traditional Olympian gods, as well as the deification of worthy humans, but Plato has a much richer theology than even this. The stars are gods as well, whose regular motion is evidence of their intelligence and eternal life. Perhaps it will strike you as even more peculiar that the entire cosmos has a soul. This makes the universe itself into a god. Some of the motivations as to why Plato posited this "world-soul" are that the universe is well-ordered and maintains that order, and is a reflection of a divine archetype.

The Demiurge

The concept of the world-soul is introduced in the *Timaeus*. In that dialogue Plato also introduced the Demiurge. A "demiurge," in Greek, is simply someone who "works for the people." He was a skilled workman of various kinds. But in *Timaeus* the Demiurge is rather like a god. The Demiurge fashions the pre-existent matter of the universe into the cosmos as we know it. In fact, the very word "cosmos" is something that is "arranged or ordered." It is this Demiurge who is responsible for making the world-soul along with the world. The relation of this god to the Forms is rather interesting, for it is in looking to the Forms that the Demiurge constructs the cosmos.

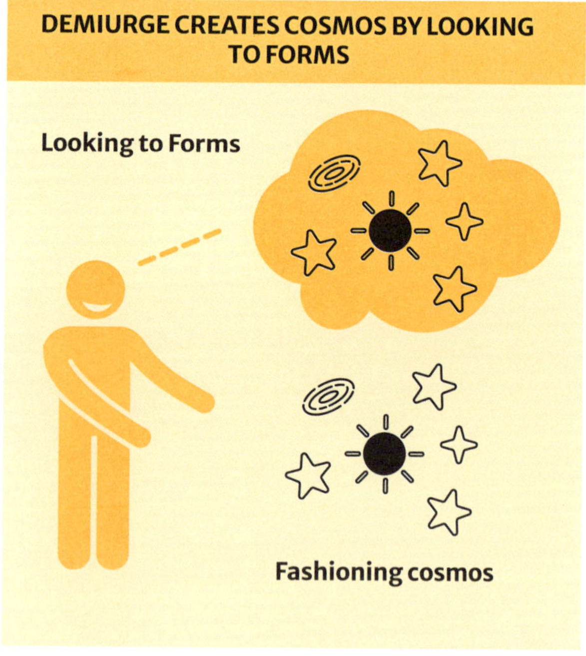

This Demiurge also fashions the gods who are to populate the heavens, the stars, made mostly of fire. These are prominent in the night sky and their divinity is evident because of their brightness. An additional point is made in the dialogue concerning the traditional gods. Remember that in the *Republic* the depiction of the gods in Homer is treated with great hostility. The *Timaeus* is by all accounts a later dialogue than the *Republic*, and the account differs in that it shifts from the characteristics of the gods to their very existence. In the *Timaeus* the emphasis is that Zeus, Hera, Aphrodite and so forth should all be believed in. The reason given is that the current occupants of Athens claim to be descendants from these people and so this is an issue of family genealogy. Even though these gods cannot be seen, they should be believed in, on the testimony of ancestors and contemporaries.

The Delphic Oracle

The most famous of all the Platonic discussions of the divine is Socrates and the Delphic Oracle. The oracle was a spokesperson for Apollo, and in the *Apology*,

Chaerophon, an associate of Socrates, was sent to query wisdom and Socrates. The question he asked was whether or not Socrates was the wisest man alive, to which the answer was yes. The famous interpretation which Socrates later gave to this report was that he was only the wisest man because he knew the wretched conditions of his own ignorance, whereas other men did not.

This brief little anecdote is a picture in miniature of some of the central themes we have discussed about the depiction of the divine in this chapter. It illustrates the relationship that Socrates and Plato both had to the traditional religion. It was reverent and observant, granting real authority to the established beliefs, as Plato and Socrates both appeared to grant legitimacy to Apollo and to his spokeswoman, the Pythian priestess. But the interpretation of what was uttered by the oracle, that Socrates was the wisest man alive, still had to be secured. In this we see a microcosm of the Platonic tendency to reform religion, for it was only after Socrates had exposed this utterance to his own experience that he came to understand its significance. Whether one calls this a reform of the

old religion or a refashioning, or even just plain pious obedience, it is clear that both Socrates and Plato took a deep interest in religious observance that took account of contemporary religious practice.

Piety and Impiety in the *Laws*

The *Laws* is Plato's last and longest work. In Book X a number of ideas and legislation are put forth to combat impiety and increase piety to the gods. There are three kinds of atheism, according to the Athenian Stranger, the main character in the dialogue. The first is a denial that the gods exist, the second is that the gods exist but do not care what humans do or do not do, and the third variety of atheism is to say the gods do exist, and pay attention to what we do, but that they can be bribed to overlook our transgressions by sacrifices and supplications.

THREE KINDS OF ATHEISM

- **Denial that the gods exist.**
- **Denial that the gods care about human affairs.**
- **Denial that the gods are just because they can be bribed by sacrifices and supplications.**

The degree to which the denial of the gods results in actual behavior is the chief concern here. The order in which I have described these three kinds of atheism is the order in which the dialogue presents them and the second and third categories of atheism can be read as interacting with the first in an interesting way. So the atheism that says the gods are indifferent to human behavior is compatible with the notion that the gods do not exist—that is, if the gods do not exist then they certainly do not care what you do! Likewise, with the third category of atheists who think they can placate the gods with sacrifices, it's as if the gods do not exist because their supervision over human affairs is nullified by after-the-fact bribes.

The Power of Religious Myth

The *Republic* and *Laws* both place emphasis on the power of tradition to enact piety in a religious people for the betterment of a city. In the *Laws* the religious obedience of the people works hand in hand with the legislative aims of the state. We will see in the chapter on the Myth of Metals in the *Republic* (Chapter 11) that raising the people of a city with a myth about their common origin helps to cement social roles and furthers group adhesion. The role that theology plays, as the proper study of the gods and our relationship to them, is almost unthinkable in the modern world, but it is a helpful example to appreciate the interconnected way that Plato sees the different areas of philosophy working together.

Chapter 10

THE GOOD

"God knows whether this happens to be true. The way things seem to me appear to be like this. In the realm of the intelligible the Form of the Good is seen last and with difficulty, and all must conclude that when it has been seen this Form of the Good is the cause of all that is right and noble..."

Republic 517b3–c1

The Allegory of the Cave (quoted opposite) is Plato's most famous passage in his most famous work. If you have not read this remarkable passage found at the beginning of *Republic* Book 7, you should, in order to appreciate its full scope and beauty. By looking to the allegory, this will set us up for understanding the concept of the good. The allegory, in large part, sets up an image of the good, and by looking at this image the concept of the good will become easier to understand.

As these men are shackled in place they are subjected to shadows of various objects, the originals of which are out of view and behind them, projected from the light of torches. This procession changes so that the dancing shadows on the wall change as well. Now what happens is that these prisoners come to associate reality with these shadows and these dancing shadows on the walls account for the whole of their experience. In order to realize their pitiful and erroneous state of ignorance these prisoners must be freed, and in coming up and out of the cave, be illumined by the light of the sun. In the light of the

"Imagine people in an underground cave-like house and it has a spread-out entrance running along the length of the cave. The people have had shackles on their legs and throats since their youth so that they stay in one place seeking only what is directly before them, and their heads are unable to rotate because of the bonds. But there is a light of fire for them coming from above and it burns at a distance. In between the fire and the people in bonds there is a path on top, along which imagine a wall, just as a screen is set before the puppet masters above which they show the puppets. Imagine next along this wall there are people holding all kinds of implements over the wall, statues of men and other stone and wood animals worked in a variety of materials. And some of the people holding the implements are uttering sounds, while others are silent."

Republic, 514a3–515a3

The Allegory of the Cave shows us the conditions of our ignorance and the revolution in understanding to overcome our ignorance.

sun things are shown for what they actually are and the prisoners' previous understanding of what they thought real is proved totally wrong. Inside the cave the prisoners were totally misinformed about the nature of reality. Being shackled and being subjected to the bizarre shadow puppets' shadows were, of course, great causes of the prisoners' ignorance. But ultimately the prisoners' main problem is not what they were subjected to but deprived of. The prison of the cave shut them off from the light of the sun, but the sun is all they really needed to show them the truth of how things really are.

In the allegory we see the central role that the sun plays. It illuminates our understanding (if we imagine ourselves in the role of the prisoners). But there is an equally and arguably more important role that the sun plays in the allegory, and that is in so far as the sun is the source of all other goodness.

The Form of the Good as the Sun

In the quotation on page 163 the "Form of the Good" is represented as the sun in the allegory. But this is where, on Plato's telling, the explanation becomes

The sun is the ultimate metaphor of knowledge and being.

familiar. The sun as a source of illumination and sight in our physical world is familiar. The Good is the cause of all that is correct and beautiful in anything. In saying this Plato is drawing our attention to the distinction between the intelligible and visible realms which we saw in Chapter 8. The sun makes things physically visible, but there is also a way in which the sun makes things visible in their goodness, meaning that the sun grants them their goodness. The sun, as the quotation makes clear, stands in for the Form of the Good.

So there is a Form of the Good which stands above and beyond everything else, bestowing goodness on everything that is good, and allowing us to see the things that are good. This Form of the Good is ultimate in several different ways. One is that every other thing that is good is sought only for the sake of this ultimate Good. Every other good is a good only because it can be used as an instrument to acquire this ultimate Good, and only the Good itself has the property of being good intrinsically. To make this more concrete, one can choose to adopt a dog, and perhaps one thinks that in so doing this "fills out the house," and one can further ask why a full house is desirable, and the answer is a happy life. In this scenario, the "happy life" is what is driving our decisions—it is this good which determines if our buying a dog or acquiring a house is good because it furthers this aim. Now, it turns out that the "happy

life" is not what Plato means by the Good, but the principle still stands: what is more derivatively a good serves to advance the cause of what is more ultimately good.

The Good and its Identity

In *Philebus*, there are extended discussions of the nature of the Good. What comes out of the discussion is that the good is accompanied by certain features. The dialogue contains a set of criteria to find the Good and a set of distinctives of the Good, and in each set there are three. The triad of criteria to find the good are desirability, sufficiency, and perfection. The triad of distinctives of the Good are beauty, measure, and truth. These distinctives are not themselves the Good, but if we see them together, we will know that whatever it is that possesses all of them is the Good. Its exact nature is certainly quite different than anything we can fully understand, and most likely anything we can even partially understand. We need these distinctives to orient us toward the Good, while being satisfied we will never quite wrap our minds around the Good.

TRIAD OF CRITERIA TO FIND THE GOOD	
Desirability	Desired more than all
Sufficiency	Lacks nothing internally
Perfection	Grants fullness externally

Desirability

If we look to the nature of the Good itself we say that the Good is desired because it is good, and that what is bad is shunned because it is bad. In other words, it is not because we desire it that something becomes good, but only as we are able to recognize the nature of a good as good that it becomes worthy of our choice.

If you remember back in the chapter on Love (Chapter 2), we also found out that people desire the Good (in that dialogue, beauty) and so to possess it forever. That analysis was in part a perspective of human psychology, and how we think and act. But there is another side to this story, focusing more on the nature of the Good and less on the human mind.

If there are many things that are good, and this seems to be the case, there is the further difficulty of determining which, if any, of these competing goods, is the ultimate Good. In *Philebus*, a distinction is made between what we can call intrinsic and instrumental goods, which we discussed earlier. Instrumental goods are only valued in so far as they serve as a road through which we must travel to reach a given goal. Intrinsic goods are those which are sought for their own sake. Ultimately, the conviction exists that there is a single intrinsic good, the Good, for the sake of which all other goods are ordered. It is this Good alone that all seek, and whatever it is that satisfies this ultimate desire is the Good.

Sufficiency

One aspect that comes out of that discussion is that the Good is sufficient. It lacks nothing, and in this sense is perfect, it is complete. The Good is that which completes everything else because it is itself already complete. This is one reason why the good man will not worry about the various trials and difficulties faced in this life. These evils do not ultimately affect the Good itself which he desires. Loss of fortune or even of life cannot change the good man, just like the Good itself is independent of needing anything else.

Perfection

The Good is perfect as well, being comprehensive in itself. Perfection in this Platonic sense is similar to sufficiency, in that perfection involves possession of everything, or at least everything worth possessing. Perfection in this way is without any lack—to be perfect is to have sufficiency turned outward, as contrasted with the inward focus of sufficiency. There is a plurality of many different kinds of things in the world which are good, and it is the perfection of the Good which brings this about. Perfection can be stated differently as fullness. A fullness which possesses what is necessary, what is wise, what is beautiful—in short, whatever is fitting for whatever circumstances we are discussing.

THE SECOND TRIAD OF DISTINCTIVES OF THE GOOD

Beauty

Measure

Truth

Beauty and Measure

In *Philebus* Plato also tells us about beauty, measure, and truth, three distinctives closely associated with the Good, to add to desirability, sufficiency, and perfection.

"If we are unable to hunt down the Good in a single idea, let us hunt it with three ideas, with beauty, measure and truth."

Philebus, 65a1–2

Beauty is understood as the proper measure of things in the proper way. This proportion of beauty is not necessarily mathematical, though it can be expressed mathematically. And because beauty is a kind of measure, this means that it is not bound by what can be seen. The easiest example of this is music, which is measured in sound.

Note that we have discussed beauty and measure together. This is because it is very difficult to separate these distinctives of the Good. A similar thing can be said of perfection and sufficiency; sufficiency is a kind of perfection, and perfection is a manner of sufficiency. Going back to the first chapter we also remember that beauty is something that is desirous. We desire beauty so strongly that we wish to possess it forever. In fact it would be hard to find one of the five other distinctives that would not be desirous all by itself. Truth and perfection seem especially desirable.

Truth

The Good is true and truth. This implies, of course, that what is false is bad, and what is bad is false. The Good is more substantial than what is bad, in that it precedes what is bad in nature. Whatever is true, to the degree it is true, is good. But this does not mean

Philosophical discussion seeks the good
through beauty, measure, and truth.

everything is equally good. Some things depend on others for their truth, such as facts of history or anything in the world of changing appearances, for that matter. But mathematical truths, or truths of logic, or moral insight, or the immortality of the soul, all of these are things that necessarily do not change and are in their goodness and truth superior to things that do change.

These different distinctives of the Good implicate one another, as we have seen. In our particular discussion of the Good itself, these distinctives can be somewhat difficult to understand because they are abstracted from our common experience and use of the term "good." Perhaps the easiest way to fold desirability, perfection, sufficiency, beauty, measure, and truth into our conception of Goodness is to acknowledge that anything that we deem good is going to possess one or perhaps several of these traits, but only Goodness itself will possess all of them.

In both Chapter 2, on Love and Chapter 4, on Elenchus, we have seen that the prospect of the Good, in all its forms, is basic to human psychological motivation. We are constantly turning our eyes and hearts to the Good. Perhaps Plato has captured something about our experience with the Good, as a frustrated search which is never fulfilled or never lasting. We get peeks through a keyhole and grasp hold for a moment, but we can never attain the full possession of what is good. We instead must make do with its emissaries, these distinctives of the Good, adequate substitutes to point us toward the way of the Good.

Chapter 11

POLITICS

"Do we say there is the justice of a single man and is there perhaps also the justice of a whole city? ... So if you want, first let us seek what kind of thing justice is in the cities. Then let us look in this way also in the case of each individual person, by looking for the likeness of the greater, the city, in the form of the lesser, the person."

Republic 368e1–369a2

Plato has a tremendous amount to say about political life, both in his masterwork *Republic* and in his latter, *Laws*, in which he amends many of his previous views set out in the *Republic*. One consistent feature of Plato's philosophy is that one field of thought brings in another. This is true in the political realm as well, where a guiding theme in the *Republic* is the relationship between the city and the soul. The structure of the soul and city match up with each other, parallel each other, and so we are able to look at either the soul or city to inform us about the other.

Politics, from this angle, is an elaboration of what it means to be human. By understanding our individual nature we come to better appreciate the nature of a human society. Furthermore, just as the parts of our soul each have their place, so too will each person find a natural place in society. The arrangement of the political order is of the utmost importance, as it determines the happiness of the citizens and the ultimate success of the city.

Life in Ancient Greece required daily involvement with the political.

The City–Soul Analogy

This beginning quotation comes in the midst of a conversation about justice. Justice is brought up by Socrates because there is a question as to whether justice will lead humans to happiness. In order to evaluate this, we must first take a closer look at justice. It turns out that "seeing" justice in the individual soul is a difficult task and so Socrates suggests comparing a soul to a city. The insights of this comparison have been conventionally referred to as the "City–Soul Analogy."

The level of correspondence between the city and the soul has been disputed by readers over the ages. This is because in the analogy Socrates suggests that the nature of the soul will be understood by looking at the nature of the city. The only assumed difference is that the city will be conveniently more understandable than the soul by itself. Because the city is bigger than a person, it will be easier to see the city's nature, just as it is easier to read larger letters than smaller letters, if the same words have been written in both. So the analogy not only concerns the city and individual soul, but also larger and smaller letters. It is a complex or double analogy.

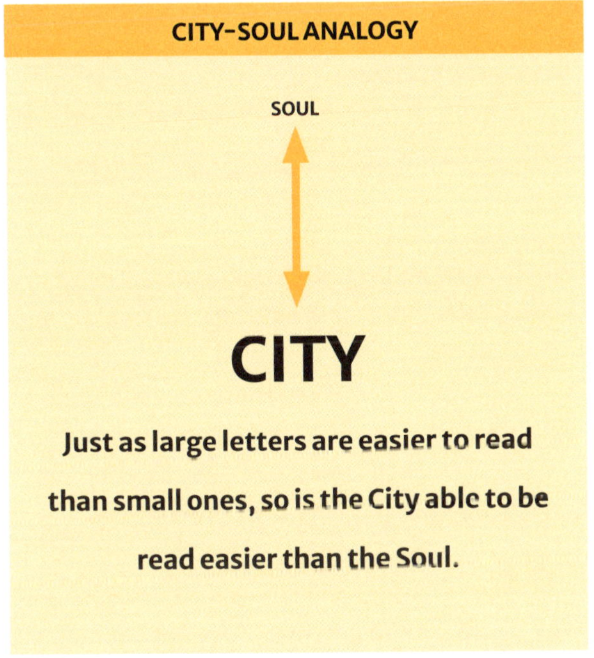

Much of the *Republic* is taken up with developing this imagined city. It is unclear, from Plato's point of view, whether this city is to be considered merely an imaginary standard or an experiment he would readily enact if given the opportunity. Socrates names this city "Kallipolis," or "Beautiful City."

Division of Labor

As with many later political accounts of the creation of society, Plato also grants that these political units come into being because of necessities which individuals alone cannot provide. There are tasks which cannot all be performed by the same person, or even if they can, they are done inadequately or perhaps even entirely neglected. There is a need for butchers, shoemakers, tailors, cooks and so forth. This division of labor requires considerable specialization in this ideal city. The focus on one's individual role is put like this by Socrates.

"The justice of the just man does not concern his actions on the outside, but the action going on inside him, that which truly concerns himself and his own things, each man not allowing himself to do anything that is not his own nor does he

allow any meddling within himself between the different parts of the soul, but truly he arranges well the things that are his own and he rules himself and orders himself and becomes a friend to himself by harmonizing the three parts of the soul."

Republic 443c–d7

This specialization will even acknowledge the political reality of war, in creating a special class of warriors whose job will be to defend the city from attacks. These warriors are to be called the "guardians." But the guardians are not to cultivate only their bodies. Their role and education is so important to the state that their personality is carefully chosen at a young age. Guardians are to have the paradoxical personality of a guard dog, which is vicious and violent toward enemies but kind and gentle toward friends.

PARADOXICAL PERSONALITY OF A GUARDIAN

Friendly to familiar

Hostile to foreign

It will turn out that this simple division between a warrior class and a worker class is not adequate for the needs of the city. The guardians will need to be assisted in their guardian tasks by a class of auxiliary helpers. The city will have a total of three class divisions: guardians, auxiliaries, and producers.

THREE IDEAL CLASSES OF THE IDEAL CITY
Guardians
Auxiliaries
Producers

Guardians

After selection as a guardian both physical and intellectual training begins. This involves gymnastics and training in different academic disciplines such as music and math, but also requires that the affections of children are correctly trained, meaning that they are raised with the correct moral emphasis. Because of this emphasis, Homer is metaphorically banished from the state, because his poetry portrays the gods as authors of evil; deceitful, adulterous, and changeable. This is unsuitable for all people, but especially for the education of the guardians. The image of the guard dog will be a good guide, a picture in a nutshell, to understand the guardian. The guardian both has to defend the city from enemies with his bodily strength and nurture the virtue and habits of citizens through care and intelligence. In brief, the guardian class is in charge of the entire welfare of the state.

Auxiliaries

Auxiliaries are in a sense nothing more than a division of the guardians, whose entire purpose is to do nothing else but help to carry out the aims and duties of the guardians. They too are compared to dogs, just as the guardians. If the guardians are to serve the state as a guard dog, then the auxiliaries serve this same role, but more directly in service and obedience to the guardians.

Producers

This class includes more or less every kind of person who is not a guardian or auxiliary. Farmers,

Auxiliary (left) and guardian (right), in Plato's conception.

manual laborers, skilled tradespeople, and artisans fit under this heading. This class produces what is necessary for the life of the city, and importantly, supports others in the producer class, as well as the guardians and auxiliaries. There is nothing especially new in Plato's introduction of this class, but its necessity makes it important for the formation of an ideal state.

Plato's idea of the producer, growing crops and cultivating wine.

The Soul and the State

To return to the City-Soul Analogy again, one of the reasons, along with perceived necessity, that Plato introduced the three-fold division of classes, was that this number corresponds to the division of the soul. From Chapter 5 we remember that the soul is divided into the logical, spirited, and appetitive parts. The City-Soul Analogy holds that by looking to the city we can see the soul, but more easily. And even in the relatively more difficult case of determining the makeup of the soul, the *Republic* has made the case that it possesses this three-fold makeup. There is a further correspondence we need to make between the parts of the soul and the classes of the city, and also the classes of the city and the virtues. (Remember, we started off the *Republic* as an inquiry into justice, one of the Greek virtues.)

The Soul and City in Parallel

The logical part of the soul corresponds to the guardian class, the spirited part to the auxiliary class and the appetitive to the producer class. Just as in the corresponding parts of the soul the spirited part helps the logical, in the city the auxiliary class supports the guardian class. Now, precisely because this ideal state is now complete, and all of the interlocutors have agreed on the various ideas which form this imaginary city, the city can be deemed "good." In the Greek context, this means it must necessarily possess the four cardinal virtues of wisdom, courage, temperance, and justice. So justice is found in this city, but how can it be determined which element is justice? Socrates proposes that if they can determine what wisdom, courage, and temperance in the city are, then justice must be whatever is left over.

Three Parts of the Soul	Three Classes of the City
Logical	Guardian
Spirited	Auxiliary
Appetitive	Producers

Finding Justice

Wisdom is found explicitly in the guardian class, while courage can be seen in the guardians and auxiliaries, and temperance, control over pleasures and passions, comes about when the guardian and auxiliary classes rightly control the producer class. This leaves justice as the only virtue as yet undefined. Justice, it is settled on, is each person performing the role he must for the benefit of the state. Justice is the condition or ability for the other three virtues to come into existence by guaranteeing they do, by ensuring each class does what it ought, and continues to do so.

The Three Waves

Plato recognizes that many of his proposals are radical shifts in the political order, and there are three proposals in particular that rise to significance. Because of this Socrates uses a metaphor to unveil these increasingly more shocking revelations. He refers to these ideas as "waves," implying that they will serve as threatening dangers to his interlocutors who will have to swim through them without being overcome and drowned.

THREE WAVES OF RADICAL POLICY

- **Women will be part of the guardian class.**
- **Women and children will be held in common.**
- **The city will be ruled by philosopher-kings.**

The first wave is that women will be included in the guardian class. This is shocking because it was thought obvious at the time that military roles should be male only. Socrates argues that women have the same type of soul as men, and are quite capable of becoming wise advisors of the guardian class. Socrates wants female guardians to have the full training and duties of their male counterparts, in accordance with their ability. He grants that they are generally physically weaker than their male counterparts. His point is that just because some women are capable of less than men, that does not mean that they can do nothing at all as a guardian.

The second wave is the elimination of the nuclear family as we know it. Instead, on the principle that friends have all things in common, all women and children are to be common property of all the men. This intermingling of sexual relations is meant to foster an equality of sentiment among all the citizens. The motivation behind this policy is that if you do not know who your son or brother is, you will treat all your fellow citizens as sons and brothers. This second wave is part of a broader eugenic movement in Plato's *Republic*. Weak or deformed children are to be killed by exposure to better the stock from which the future generations will be born.

The last, and most difficult of all the waves to survive, is the idea of the philosopher-king. This is nothing less than a combination of the art of politics and the knowledge of philosophy. These two disparate fields must be taken up in the person of a philosopher-king, who alone has the ability to steer the ship of state properly.

The policies of Plato's ideal state are clearly meant

to maximize the Good for the state as a whole, with little concern for the individual aims of citizens. If personal life goals come into view at all, these happen only incidentally. The betterment of the city must come first, and it is only within their proper class, and role within that class, that citizens have the freedom to do what they please.

The philosopher-king.

The Myth of the Metals

In order to educate the populace in a way which will both ingrain and reinforce the tri-partition of society into three classes, Socrates proposes a so-called Myth of Metals. This myth, to be related to the citizens from birth, will state that they all spring from the earth, and that the guardians are born with gold inside of them, auxiliaries with silver and producers with bronze. Socrates imagines addressing the people of his imaginary city in this way.

"All of you are brothers in this city, but for as many of you as are fitted to rule, he mixed gold in them at their creation, because they are the most valued. And as many as are auxiliaries, he mixed silver in with them. And he mixed in iron and bronze into the farmers and all the other workers."

Republic 415a2–8

This myth will make it natural to accept a role in one of the three classes, and it also shows how Plato conceived of the classes as a hierarchy, with the guardians most valuable.

The unity of the state must be believed in at a personal level, and something like a religious conviction is required for buy-in from all the members of that society. The ideal state is brought into realization not through coercion but through the unifying power of a national mythos. In Plato's political imagination we are exposed to a wide range of ideas which he explored and developed. In Plato the political involves all other elements of philosophy. The political is entirely philosophical.

Happiness

This right ordering of the state, with the appropriate and necessary classes, constitutes justice. Since justice manifests only when the other three virtues of wisdom, courage, and temperance have come into being, the city has a completeness with justice. With the completeness of the city also comes happiness. The city with wisdom, courage, temperance, and justice has achieved happiness by the correct division of classes working for the good of the whole city. This is also the case for the individual soul, which achieves happiness only by the right relationship between the three parts of the soul analogous to the city.

Chapter 12

CONCLUSION

“These sentences contain the culture of nations; these are the corner-stone of schools; these are the fountain-head of literatures. Plato is philosophy, and philosophy, Plato.”

Ralph Waldo Emerson

The influence of Plato, like few thinkers in the history of the world, is immeasurable. Many different fields, people, and ideas have been inspired by his writing. This is not only because of the breadth of his interests, but also the depths to which he explored them. The open-ended nature of the dialogues leads a reader to imaginative thinking.

The topics we have read about in these chapters have set the table for philosophical discussions for the past two millennia. Some of the themes have obvious application to everyday human cares: love, the soul, ethics or how to act, the divine, politics. Others, even though they seem more remote from our experience, find parallels or applications in modern day settings. So the Theory of Forms concerns how we think about and know things, and the identification of virtue with knowledge gives us a reason to be informed in what we believe and about why we act as we do. Even the height of Plato's philosophical abstractions, his concept of the Good, has real relevance to our pursuit of what is good in both the short term and over the whole of our lives.

Plato's Legacy

In the immediate aftermath of Plato's death, his academy passed on to his nephew, Speussipus. The Academy, in different forms, with different emphases, persisted for centuries. Of particular interest, the Academy fluctuated between a rigid dogmatism of what Plato taught, or what it was believed he taught, and an uncommitted sceptical orientation. The head of the Academy, changing from time to time, determined this trajectory. Aristotle, in charge of his own institute, the Lyceum, continued on a broadly Platonic research course, often engaging the same topics, sometimes with more detail but just as often disagreeing with his master, such as on the nature of Forms or the best form of political constitution.

Plato's influence was bound up with that of Socrates, because judging by public interest, Plato's account of Socrates was the most compelling of all the doings and sayings of Socrates, even though other writers, like Xenophon, took their own crack at the task of Socratic chronicling. Socrates was also a revered figure in the school of Stoicism.

Epicurus, founder of Epicureanism, was clearly well-read in Plato's theorizing on pleasure and arguments about the soul, since he engaged Platonic-leaning ideas directly despite no explicit acknowledgement of his sources.

The subsequent history of Greek and Roman philosophy is a story of the reception of Plato, through his Socrates, and by way of his most famous pupil, Aristotle. Plato was so formidable that engagement with his philosophy was necessary if one were to engage in any philosophy at all, whether that meant agreement or disagreement. On the critical side this meant that the views expressed in Plato's dialogues became commonplaces, a currency to refer to philosophical ideas in a similar way in which today someone can quote a character from a movie, bringing to mind the entirety of the scene. Not everything in Plato is easy or clear, however, and so there was a development of competing views of what Plato said. This eventually lead to ancient commentators and commentaries on dialogues that have survived until today. Their very existence tells us that there was an appetite for an explanation of what Plato meant and a philosophically curious community from which this demand was coming.

One of the more notable schools of Platonic thought came about in later antiquity. This school has been dubbed 'neo-Platonic,' for it was a kind of new revival of Plato, steering philosophy into a devoted attention to Platonic writing and emphasizing the mystical and religious aspects of Plato. The head of this movement was Plotinus (AD 204/205–270), whose own writings and that of his pupils were to exert a large influence on St. Augustine (AD 354–430), the philosopher-theologian so important to the nascent Christian church. In St. Augustine there is a noticeable fusion of faith and philosophy, whose philosophical contributions help to set off the Middle Ages.

Throughout the continued history of the West, Plato has played an immense part. Of course, with Aristotle, Plato played a large part in medieval philosophy, though it was largely through his dialogue *Timaeus*, on the nature and origin of the universe, that medieval Latin thinkers engaged with Plato. The theological parallels, adapted to Christian understanding, made the dialogue a compelling focus of scrutiny and speculation. Thomas Aquinas (1225–1274), although famously adapting the philosophy of Aristotle, probably took as much or even more, from Plato's thinking in his theology.

It would take until the time of Marsilio Ficino (1433–1499), that the West was completely exposed to the fullness of Plato's works after the neglect he had seen for centuries. Ficino's translation of Plato's complete works were printed in 1484, and their dissemination into the scholarly language of Latin did much to re-popularize and encourage the 'rediscovery' of Plato.

Another hallmark for the reception of Plato in the West was René Descartes (1596–1650). Clearly engaging with and reacting to ideas first found in Plato, Descartes is most famous for his identification of the self with the rational part of the soul, and a hard distinction between the body and the soul. The soul, its existence and its nature has been a point of increasing contention since Descartes' day.

Perhaps the next most monumental period that Plato influenced was the rise of Idealism. Two figures associated with this movement are George Berkeley (1685–1753) and Immanuel Kant (1724–1804). Plato's Theory of Forms, prioritizing an invisible and intellectually accessible realm, was a necessary precursor to Idealism. Idealism, without abolishing the key thinkers which held to different versions of it, posits that something dependent on or identical with the mind serves as the basis of reality, and that reality can only be known through the mind rather than through the experience of external objects.

Now there are many other influences that Plato has had through the centuries, but these are some of the most prominent and consequential. Plato's ideas, refuted or accepted, are never unchanged. This owes to the richness of the Platonic dialogues, but also indicates that adaption, borrowing, 'improving,' rejecting and combining Plato's ideas with new ones has always been a feature of the reception of this philosopher. Plato is the father of philosophy as well as the father of many philosophers. When we read Plato, we are not only reading him, but everyone who has previously read him along with us, taking their interpretations and their joy in reading him.

Index